CROSSED SIGNALS

HOW TO SAY
NO
TO SEXUAL HARASSMENT

CROSSED SIGNALS

HOW TO SAY **NO**
TO SEXUAL HARASSMENT

by Memory VanHyning

Foreword by Debra Borys, Ph.D.

INFOTRENDS PRESS
P.O. Box 25356
Los Angeles, CA 90025-0356

CROSSED SIGNALS

How to say NO to Sexual Harassment

by Memory VanHyning

Published by
Infotrends Press
P.O. Box 25356
Los Angeles, CA 90025-0356

Copyright © 1993 by Memory VanHyning and J.M. Glasc, Inc.
First printing 1993

Printed in the United States of America.
Library of Congress Catalog Card Number: 92-74742
ISBN: 1-882562-00-3

Contributors:	Debra Borys, Ph.D.
	Tibor Jukelevics, Ph.D.
Editorial Advisor:	Judith L. Cole
Development Editor:	Deborah Grandinetti
Production Editor:	Susan Leavitt Meisel
Book/cover design:	Carolyn Porter and Todd Meisler
	One-On-One Book Production

For my mother,
Frances,
who blazed a path for me.

For my friend,
Judy,
who joined me on the trail.

And for my son,
Rory,
who I hope will find
the journey less bewildering.

TABLE OF CONTENTS

SECTION I: WHAT IS SEXUAL HARASSMENT?

SECTION II: HOW TO SAY NO

SECTION III: WHEN WORDS FAIL

SECTION IV: LOOKING FORWARD

APPENDICES

PREFACE

I've encountered sexual harassment most of my working life. I wish I could say I always handled it well, but the truth is, like most women, I often chose to ignore it, blame myself or seethe in silence. I wish I had known then what I know now: *you CAN say no to sexual harassment and still keep your dignity, your self-esteem, and your job.*

My years of experience in the corporate training field, plus my extensive interviews with hundreds of personnel managers, corporate executives, training consultants, counselors, lawyers, and other working men and women have taught me a lot about sexual harassment. I am convinced that we're approaching the problem from the wrong direction. I think there's been too much emphasis placed on managing a crisis caused by sexual harassment and far too little on preventing it from happening in the first place.

Somehow, in our zeal to create legislation and company policy, we've forgotten the day-to-day reality of the workplace. Men and women have to work together, but they interact differently. Most of us do want to work in an environment of mutual respect and fairness, but we often struggle in communicating with one another. Although we're often unaware of it, we as individuals have more power in setting the tone for our workplace than any written policy or law—but we need to be shown how.

This book raises issues that are of interest to both men and women, but it's awkward to write about sexual harassment in gender-neutral terms, because the overwhelming majority of harassers are men and their victims are women. So while I've usually identified the harasser as "he," I don't intend this to be an indictment of men. Sexual harassment victimizes both men and women. This book is about communication and how to resolve problems caused by the mixed messages we often send to one another because of our gender.

I hope my ideas will be a valuable ally in the struggle against sexual harassment—especially for people who must face the daily battle. Ultimately, sexual harassment is not only a women's problem, but a problem men and women have to solve together.

Memory VanHyning

NOTE: *This book is not intended to be a substitute for psychological counseling or legal advice. If you feel there are unresolved issues in your life that may affect your emotional or physical health—on or off the job—I urge you to seek professional help.*

FOREWORD

by
Debra Borys, Ph.D.
Psychologist in Private Practice
Assistant Clinical Professor of Psychology, UCLA

Trapped. Powerless. These seem to be the two words women use most to describe how they feel about being sexually harassed. Why is this important? Because it is these feelings that tend to contribute to the deepest depression and the most intense physical reactions, incapacitating women at work. If a woman perceives herself as powerless to defend herself against harassment, she is unlikely to take any self-protective action. Consequently, she continues to suffer.

Why does sexual harassment make most women feel so trapped and powerless? I believe that one reason is that the harassment causes a conflict of needs—the need (and desire and *right*) to be free of degradation and of bodily violation and the need to maintain their income and job. They worry that rebuffing their harasser may affect their job security and threaten their job status.

Women tend to feel even more trapped and powerless when the harasser is someone who has authority over them, or when they are being abused by someone they have perhaps relied on for mentoring or guidance. The experience of being degraded or violated by someone in authority, particularly when it is someone you have depended upon, is akin to the same betrayal that occurs in incest.

Like incest survivors, sexual harassment survivors often *do* feel degraded, violated and betrayed. They share the same fears and sense of being "small" and vulnerable. These feelings may be especially intense if the harassment situation revives powerful and painful memories of the childhood abuse.

There is another reason why victims of sexual harassment feel so powerless, confused and vulnerable. Most people who have not experienced assault or abuse in their lives carry around a set of beliefs about justice and safety in the world. Often unconscious, these beliefs help them feel more secure and free from worry in their daily lives. These beliefs usually include:

1. *Bad things don't happen to good people. I'm a good person so bad things won't happen to me.*

2. *As long as I work hard, I'll be successful.*

3. *If I treat others with respect, they'll do the same to me.*

Sadly, the experience of sexual harassment shatters all of these beliefs: bad things like harassment *do* happen to good people; harassment can impede a woman's career no matter how hard she's worked; and treating others on the job with respect is unfortunately *not* fail-safe insurance against harassment.

This book is based on assertive communication techniques. Assertiveness involves calm, firm, factual direct, and non-attacking communication regarding one's wants, needs, and dissatisfactions. It was written to teach you practical skills to counter the dynamics of feeling paralyzed and powerless about sexual harassment. It will provide you, step by step, with ways to respond assertively to a harasser in order to end the harassment and may not affect sacrificing important work relationships or cause undue harm to your job.

The act of expressing feelings about the harassment, rather than holding them inside, can be a tremendous relief. Women who respond assertively to harassment tend to experience less depression and are less likely to become ill or experience lower self-esteem. This is true whether or not they are immediately successful in stopping the harasser.

Assertive communication is empowering, because it gives you a way to exert some positive control and influence over the situation and on the harasser's behavior. It can be self-affirming to honestly express your feelings about the harassment and request an end to it. Moreover, in most cases, assertive responses such as those suggested in this book, may effectively halt a harasser's behavior.

ACKNOWLEDGMENTS

This book combines the advice of experts in psychology and business with the experience of many people. *CROSSED SIGNALS* reflects years of listening, caring and trying to understand the problems of sexual harassment that affect so many of us in our daily lives.

I have been blessed with some wonderful friends and business associates who have been patient with me as I've researched, debated, surveyed, and struggled to make sense of my outrage over sexual harassment. Les Hajnal and Bruce Weyne of Infotrends Press especially shared my passion about finding realistic solutions to this problem. They believed so strongly in this project that they were willing to invest considerable time and resources on an untried author. Tibor Jukelevics, Ph.D., of the Center for Family in Los Angeles, was particularly helpful with his insights about victims of sexual abuse. My editor, Deborah Grandinetti, helped me realize that the passion of my beliefs could give my words real meaning, and she kept me true to that commitment.

But one person can never be thanked enough. In 1987, an enterprising and wonderfully sensitive young woman named Judith Cole, asked me to join her in launching a small company we named J. M. Glasc, Inc. Our first product, an award-winning training video for employees called "Sexual Harassment is Bad Business," changed our lives and has had an impact on the lives of thousands of workers in this country. Since that time, as business partners and friends, we've never wavered in our belief that honest communication can make a positive difference in the workplace—not only for women, but for everyone who holds a job and works with other people. I am so grateful to Judy for her special insights and her unique ability to communicate those insights to others.

If this book helps even one person conquer sexual harassment, it will have been worth the efforts of everyone who so generously contributed to its creation.

MVH
Spokane, Washington

*No one can make you feel inferior
without your consent.*
–Eleanor Roosevelt

INTRODUCTION
How This Book Can Help You

This book can help reverse the downward spiral that sexual harassment can create in your life by giving you the tools you need to change the way people treat you. It literally tells you what to say and what to do if you are threatened by sexual harassment on the job.

You'll learn how to define sexual harassment for yourself, how to recognize the type of harassing behavior you face, and how to respond to someone who is harassing you. You'll learn to assert yourself in a way that strives to maintain good working relationships with your co-workers and superiors. You'll also learn what your options are—and what risks you face—should you choose to take formal action against a harasser who refuses to stop.

Standing up for yourself has enormous benefits. You'll feel a new sense of power and self-respect that's bound to spill over into other areas of your life. You may also find that co-workers will be impressed by your confident handling of a difficult situation.

Until recently, the majority of working women have held subordinate positions in the workplace. Now women are expanding into leadership and management roles and entering nontraditional fields as well. The assertive techniques this book promotes can help you in all of these ventures.

Adding Your Personal Touch

I'd like to suggest that you use the book as both a guide and a personal journal. As you read the stories of others who have experienced sexual harassment, think about how you might react in the same situation. Imagine yourself facing that situation at work. Write down how you would respond. Then compare your response with the ones I suggest in Section Two of this book, and choose a response that is comfortable for you. Does it differ from your initial response? Can you see which one is likely to work better?

Even if the situations I describe seem remote from anything you'd experience, it's good practice to think about how you'd respond. Think of this as emotional CPR, a way of preparing yourself to respond in an "emergency." Knowing that there are things you can say—and feel comfortable saying—will give you a sense of assurance that you can meet whatever situation arises.

It Takes Practice

Like any skill, being assertive does take practice. You'll need to develop a sense of ease in using assertive responses to communicate. It is in this way that you'll overcome your fear and the sense of powerlessness that sexual harassment so often creates. With practice, you can do it.

You don't have to agree with every point to use this information to your benefit. Some of these ideas may help you discover new ones of your own, and that's great. You should adapt them to fit your own personal style and your unique work situation. You know what is right for you.

Practice With Yourself, Your Mirror, or a Friend

There are some simple, but valuable ways to practice assertive responses to sexual harassment. You can start by saying the verbal responses out loud. Read them to yourself, or use a tape recorder, or talk to your mirror. Hearing yourself say the responses helps you decide which ones work best for you. It also builds your confidence.

Next, try to practice while you're jogging or driving to work. Have "conversations" with yourself. Picture yourself handling a situation successfully. Envision the respect you'll get from others when you stand up for yourself. These are powerful images that help prepare you and strengthen your resolve.

You'll benefit greatly from role-playing these situations with a friend. Critique each other's delivery and body language. Your exchanges will build confidence. Develop your own "scripts," using the stories and responses in the book, or your own work experiences. Make the situations realistic. The more familiar you become with the responses, the more likely it is that you'll remember them, and use them effectively if the need arises.

Talk about the ideas in this book with your friends and co-workers. Talking about sexual harassment really helps build awareness and understanding. It can do much to establish a positive, healthy environment in your workplace.

There are many advantages to learning how to handle sexual harassment yourself, not the least of which is the feeling of empowerment you'll develop as a result of being more assertive. There's another important consideration you might overlook because of anger and frustration. That is: *Resolving the situation on your own may allow you and your harasser to continue to work together in ways which don't compromise your dignity or jeopardize your career.*

In Section I, you'll learn what sexual harassment is, what causes it, and the types of harassing behavior you're likely to face. In Section II, you'll learn how to assertively stand up to your harasser—including what to say, plus how and when to say it for the greatest impact.

Assertively responding to your harasser will work for you most of the time. You should be aware however, that some harassers will persist even if you assert yourself and do everything right. They may pose a threat serious enough for you to consider taking further action.

That's why I developed the information about your rights, risks, and options that you'll find in Section III. It includes candid discussions about preparing a case against your harasser, guidelines for reporting your harasser, and practical ways you can get help from your company's management, government agencies, and the legal system.

You are truly your own best defense against sexual harassment. This book can help you build the personal power to resolve most sexual harassment as soon as it starts.

Whether or not you're being harassed now, the time you spend preparing yourself to stop sexual harassment will be one of your wisest investments.

NELDA'S STORY

He was my first boss. He kept asking me out and I said no every time. Then he started leaving messages on my voice mail...things with all kinds of sexual innuendoes. I told him to stop it, but they just kept getting more and more explicit. Every time I had to have some kind of contact with him at work, he'd try to make it into something else. He'd say things like "I know why you're in here—you've finally decided to let a real man show you how to make your life complete." I worked for this guy—how was I supposed to get the work done without talking to him?

Finally, I'd just had it with the whole situation. I went in and told him I was quitting, and he was absolutely shocked. He couldn't believe how upset I was by what he claimed was, "just joking around." He actually thought I should be flattered by the attention! I spent the next 45 minutes letting him know exactly how it made me feel and why I couldn't work for somebody who treated me like that.

That discussion saved my job. Maybe I took a risk and maybe it could have gone the other way with somebody else, but for me, it was a turning point. If I'd said something to him months before, I could have saved both of us a lot of grief. I almost left a job that was really important to getting my career off the ground ...and he almost lost the best PR trainee he'd ever had.

SECTION I

WHAT IS SEXUAL HARASSMENT?

Chapter 1

DEFINING SEXUAL HARASSMENT

Drawing Your Own Line

B oth men and women say they're confused about how to relate to one another on the job. It seems that all the concern about sexual harassment has put new restrictions on us. After all, men and women are different, so it's no surprise that we interpret things differently. Some people say they just don't know what constitutes appropriate behavior in the workplace. They want someone to define sexual harassment for them, and help them recognize when the "line" has been crossed.

The fact is, most of us already know when our personal line is crossed, and we know how to recognize sexual harassment. A 1992 *Working Woman* survey found that 80% of us know it by its legal definition or intuitively understand it when it happens to us.

If you feel unclear, read the legal definition below. Then consider the "Four-Question Reality Check," a list of questions that will help you determine for yourself if a particular behavior meets the criteria of the law.

Of course, you have the right to express your dislike of any unwanted behavior that creates a hostile work environment for you, whether or not it fits the legal definition of sexual harassment. No one else can decide that for you.

It makes sense to take the time to define for yourself what you will and will not accept at work, especially with regard to flirting; sexually-oriented photos, drawings, jokes; sexually-oriented conversation, gestures, or touching. Defining your position before you find yourself in an uncomfortable situation gives you the advantage. Knowing what your boundaries are, you'll be quicker to speak up for yourself when someone crosses the line.

What the Law Says

Sexual harassment is a form of sex discrimination under Title VII (703)-(704a) of the Civil Rights Act of 1964, as amended. Sexual harassment complaints are under the jurisdiction of the Equal Employment Opportunity Commission. This is the official EEOC definition:

Unwelcome sexual advances, requests for sexual favors, and other verbal or physical conduct of a sexual nature constitute sexual harassment when:

1. Submission to such conduct is made either explicitly or implicitly a term or condition of an individual's employment.

2. Submission to or rejection of such conduct by an individual is used as the basis for employment decisions affecting such individual.

3. Such conduct has the purpose or effect of unreasonably interfering with an individual's work performance; or creating an intimidating, hostile, or offensive working environment.

3

The law also assigns specific responsibility, or liability, to the employer:

An employer is generally responsible for its acts and those of its agents and supervisory employees with respect to sexual harassment regardless of whether the specific act complained of was authorized or even forbidden by the employer and regardless of whether the employer knew or should have known of its occurrence.

With respect to conduct between fellow employees, an employer is generally responsible for acts of sexual harassment in the workplace where the employer, its agents or supervisory employees, knows or should have known of the conduct, unless it can show that it took immediate and appropriate corrective action.

An employer may also be responsible for the acts of non-employees, with respect to sexual harassment of employees in the workplace, where the employer, its agents or supervisory employees, knows or should have known of the conduct and fails to take immediate and appropriate corrective action.

Prevention is the best tool for elimination of sexual harassment. An employer should take all steps necessary to prevent sexual harassment from occurring, such as affirmatively raising the subject, expressing strong disapproval, developing appropriate sanctions, informing employees of their right to raise and how to raise the issue of harassment, and developing methods to sensitize all concerned.

Where employment opportunities or benefits are granted because of an individual's submission to the employer's sexual advances or requests for sexual favors, the employer may be held liable for unlawful sex discrimination against other persons who were qualified for, but denied that employment opportunity or benefit.

What the Law Means

It may sound pretty complex, but it's actually quite simple: *Sexual harassment is any sexually-oriented conduct on the job that is unwelcome, unwanted, and offensive to the recipient, and which may negatively affect the recipient's job performance.*

How unwelcome, how unwanted, and how offensive is pretty much up to you. Some states have gone a step further in attempting to clarify this by applying what is called the "reasonable person," or more recently, the "reasonable woman" standard. This means that the degree of offensiveness is measured by what a "reasonable" person or woman would consider offensive.

NOTE: *Laws in some states interpret sexual harassment differently.*

The Four-Question Reality Checks

The following questions can help you decide for yourself if what you're experiencing is sexual harassment. If you answer any of these questions "yes," then you can consider that the "line" has been crossed: *Is it real? Is it related? Is it rejected? Is it repeated?*

1. Is it REAL?

Did I hear it correctly? Is this something I find offensive? Does this really have the meaning I think it did? Was it addressed to me in a personal way? If you're uncertain, ask the person who made the statement what he meant by it.

2. Is it RELATED?

Does it have something to do with my job or the way I do my work? Will it affect the way I feel about my work or keep me from doing my job? Sometimes we have a hard time separating social behavior from work behavior when we feel comfortable with a person, but there's a crucial difference. If the unwelcome behavior is job-related, it is a protected situation under the law.

3. Is it REJECTED?

Do I want this behavior to stop?

Honestly assess your feelings about the other person and the situation. Have you accepted this behavior from one person but not another? Are you being ultra-sensitive because of other feelings that may be involved? Have you made it clear to the person that you do not welcome this kind of behavior?

4. Is it REPEATED?

Has this happened before with this person? Is it part of a pattern? Is it happening again after you've asked for it to stop? It's important to make a distinction between something that's just happened for the first time and something that's happened several times. Although discriminatory behavior is unlawful even if it happens only once, most people consider sexual harassment unwelcome behavior *that is repeated*. It's not a first-time remark or action, unless, of course, it involves offenses such as intentional or overt caressing of genitals or breasts, self-exposure, or sexual assault.

Evaluating Your Answers

This four-question process can help you assess situations logically and to document them clearly. Answering each of these questions helps you be more objective and less emotional. This will help give you more credibility when you stand up to your harasser or report the situation.

Conversely, this four-question process may also spare you the embarrassment of accusing someone of sexual harassment when that wasn't the intent at all. Why risk your job or reputation, or someone else's, needlessly?

Considering the behavior or remark in its overall context is a helpful way to determine whether it really deserves your concern. Did it occur in the workplace, or at a social gathering, like the company picnic or an office party? Did alcohol cause a slip of the tongue?

Could it be the pressure of tight deadlines, on-site skill testing, or an upcoming client presentation that's causing the individual to act or speak thoughtlessly? Again, consider: Is this a one-time bit of foolishness that isn't likely to be repeated, or is it something that continues to undermine your comfort at work? Be aware of the difference.

IS IT SEXUAL HARASSMENT?
Crossing the Line

If you're uncertain whether you should let a remark or behavior go unchallenged, these questions may help you:

- Is this joke/behavior/conversation inappropriate to the relationship?
- Is this relationship inappropriate for work?
- Would my colleagues consider this unprofessional behavior?
- Would I feel uncomfortable if my spouse/companion/ child/friend overheard this remark?
- Could this be misinterpreted by others who don't know the situation?

Chapter 2

THE REALITY OF TODAY'S WORKPLACE

After Thomas & Hill: Has Anything Changed?

S exual harassment awareness did not arrive in America compliments of Clarence Thomas and Anita Hill. No matter how shocked members of the United States Senate Judiciary Committee appeared to be by Professor Hill's allegations, most of us are not so naive about sexual harassment in the workplace. Whether or not the University of Oklahoma law professor's story was believed by the Senators, it rang true enough for millions of American working women.

Anita Hill's testimony focused the nation's attention on the problem that an estimated 65 percent[1] of working women will encounter—sexual harassment on the job. Anita Hill's testimony also sparked

---

1. Depending on the survey taken, the industry studied, the percentage of women in the sample group, how questions were asked, when the survey was taken, and how the results were compiled. I have seen figures on the incidence of sexual harassment range from less than 25% to over 90% of the working population. There is no consensus as to the exact percentage.

much debate about how to effectively eliminate sexual harassment from the workplace.

Has It Made Any Difference?

It depends upon whom you ask.

In a 1992 follow-up of its original 1988 report on "Sexual Harassment in the Fortune 500," *Working Woman* magazine found that 80 percent of the companies surveyed said they now had programs to combat sexual harassment.[2] That figure was up from 60 percent in 1988.

But how effective were these programs? Executives responsible for handling sexual harassment complaints said that 80 to 90 percent of the cases were handled fairly. *Working Woman's* readers disagreed. Only 21 percent of that group said that they believed complaints overall were handled fairly. Another 60 percent of those readers said that they felt charges of sexual harassment were completely ignored.

This is unfortunate, because it implies that millions of workers vulnerable to sexual harassment in the workplace have little faith in their employer's commitment—or ability—to do anything about it. According to Dr. Barbara Gutek, a psychologist and one of the pioneering researchers in the field, sex at work is "a problem for half of all workers, and not surprisingly, for many more women than men."

---

2. "Sexual Harassment in the Fortune 500," 1988, and "Sexual Harassment: The Inside Story," *Working Woman* , 1988, 1992.

In her book, *Sex And The Workplace: The Impact of Sexual Behavior and Harassment on Women, Men and Organizations,* Dr. Gutek notes that "...it is a mistake to assume that none of it (i.e., sexual harassment) has work-related consequences."[3] Her research has led her to conclude that sexual harassment is common in virtually every workplace environment.

Just how common has yet to be documented with any real accuracy. In 1990, 5,550 victims of sexual harassment in the U.S. were adamant enough to file a formal complaint against their employer with the Equal Employment Opportunity Commission.[4] The EEOC anticipates receiving at least twice that number of complaints by the end of this year, an increase that shows no signs of declining. Yet these numbers represent only a tiny percentage (less than 5%) of those victimized by sexual harassment. Many more individuals presumably suffer in silence, quit their jobs or ask for transfers. Too few seem able to achieve satisfaction by working within company channels.

Who are These Victims?

Victims of sexual harassment include men and women, although only about 8% of the cases reported actually involve a man being harassed by a woman or another

---

3. Gutek, Barbara. *Sex and the Workplace: The Impact of Sexual Behavior and Harassment on Women, Men, and Organizations.* San Francisco, Jossey-Bass, 1985.

4. Based on agency reports for 1990, the latest year for which data was available, only 51 of more than 5,500 cases reported for that year were litigated by the EEOC.

11

man. Older women are not exempt, but younger women are the more frequent targets. Women who are single, separated, divorced or living with someone seem to be the most vulnerable, according to Dr. Gutek.

Studies have also found that women with advanced education are particularly vulnerable because their career paths may be more dependent upon a particular job. In fact, female managers are slightly more likely than any other group of working women to be harassed.

The indirect victim of sexual harassment is the corporation itself. Sexual harassment lowers productivity and morale while increasing absenteeism and turnover. In 1988, business consultant Freada Klein calculated that a single case of sexual harassment could cost a typical employer as much as $6.7 million dollars—and that doesn't even include the cost of defending the company if the case goes to court.[5]

Contributing Factors

Sexual harassment is part of the reality of today's workplace. Why is there so much of it? That's still being debated. My experience indicates that it often results from a breakdown in male/female communications.

Men and women tend to think and communicate differently, particularly about sex, and especially at work. The way we communicate directly affects the way we perceive each other. That perception ultimately

---

5. Freada Klein, as quoted in "Sexual Harassment in the Fortune 500," *Working Woman*, 1988.

affects our behavior and consequently, the way we treat each other. Cultural backgrounds also play a role in different ways of communicating.

Hostility and the need to control others motivates the behavior of the more dangerous perpetrators of sexual harassment. They may use the power they derive from their position in the company to humiliate their victims, and force them into having sex or leaving their jobs. This type of behavior is more common when women enter male-dominated fields such as construction or law enforcement, but it can be a problem in any organization in which women challenge traditional male roles.

Competition is a factor, too. Men and women today compete fiercely with each other for jobs, promotions, and recognition—and as always, for attention from one another. Even as there are women who "sleep their way to the top," there are also men who use sexual harassment to destroy a female colleague competing with them for advancement. Sex can be a very intimidating weapon in the power struggle.

In situations where there may be no real intent to hurt someone, confusion is often the culprit. Some individuals find working with the opposite sex highly distracting or even disorienting. Others continue to be confused about the protocol of a professional working relationship. And some think flirtatious behavior is appropriate.

Men and women are only beginning to let go of rigidly defined sex roles in order to learn how to work well together. The entry of women into male dominated workplaces is relatively recent. We bring to our jobs deeply-held convictions about ourselves, each other and our "proper roles" as men and women. Sometimes these beliefs clash sharply with the demands of the workplace. Often they clash with the ideas and experiences of others.

Psychologist Barbara Gutek calls this, "sex-role spillover." As defined in her book, *Sex and the Workplace*, "sex role spillover" refers to those sex roles men and women are expected to adopt in their personal lives. These roles "spill over" and interfere with work roles, creating inappropriate expectations.

Some men, for instance, expect women employees to act like mothers, wives or girlfriends—in other words, to be more nurturing, loyal, or dependent, than a man holding the same job. And some women feel more comfortable with traditional female roles, especially if they believe that men at work will only accept them in a more submissive or traditionally "female" role.

It's no wonder that signals get crossed. Learning to work alongside each other is not easy when the rules of behavior are in such transition. Men in the workplace are now expected to treat women seriously. Those who once placed women on pedestals are now being asked to discard these notions and treat them as equals. Those who don't are accused of being chauvinistic. Women are also redefining their roles and the behavior that's appropriate for their new responsibilities. Those who were once taught to defer to men are now trying to learn how to manage and lead them.

For women, there is even confusion about what "feminine" means in the workplace. For instance, the popular magazines that once told us how to dress for success by sublimating our more feminine aspects, now often encourage us to celebrate our femininity by expressing it in highly visible ways. While such magazines urge us to dress and act like women, they also urge us to be more like men—in our ambitions, our tenacity, our decisiveness, and especially in our detachment from emotions in decision-making. These magazines would have us follow a recipe for success that's full of jumbled ingredients and mixed messages.

As Susan Faludi points out in her book, *Backlash: The Undeclared War Against American Women*, much of this advice is a reaction against the "feminization" of the American workplace. Magazines that encourage women to take themselves seriously also carry fashion layouts featuring man-tailored pinstripe suits layered over lacy camisoles and sexy lingerie. The models are depicted as successful working women and are shown in boardrooms and office environments. They look very, very sexy. What is the message here? And for whom? Is a working woman who dresses in sexy clothes asking for trouble? While it makes sense to examine the image you may be portraying with your attire, Dr. Debra Borys notes that women who dress attractively should not assume the blame for being sexually harassed. Harassment is inappropriate and illegal behavior no matter what you are wearing.

Don't Look to Your Employer to Prevent Sexual Harassment

Given all this confusion, is it any wonder that employers often feel so uncomfortable with their

15

legally-mandated mission to prevent sexual harassment in the workplace? Since the early 1980s, when the passage of amendments to the Civil Rights Act of 1964 formally defined sexual harassment and recognized it as a type of discrimination, employers were given the responsibility for dealing with sexual harassment in the workplace. It is not a role they welcomed then or now.

Employers haven't been very successful at preventing harassment either, despite the policy statements, reporting procedures, and training sessions they've implemented over the past ten years. Companies have spent millions of dollars to reduce their liability in this area, but surveys show that the percentage of people who claim to have been victimized by sexual harassment continues to rise.

Government Can't Cope

And what about the government? Can the government do anything about sexual harassment? Well, it has done something. There is legislation on the books (and more being added every year) at federal, state and local levels prohibiting sexual harassment. There are federal and state agencies set up to provide information, regulate compliance, and gather data. To no one's surprise, there is an elaborate labyrinth of procedural bureaucracy to handle complaints.

Less than five percent of people who say they are victims of sexual harassment actually use the remedies of the law and the available resources of their state and federal governments to bring them relief. It's not only a reluctance to take formal action that limits the number of complaints being filed. Those who do file complaints to the EEOC or a state agency find funding and staff are limited. The tremendous increase in the number of cases being filed in the aftermath of the Thomas-Hill hearings have resulted in a huge backlog of cases, delays in investigations for years, and frustrations on all sides. These overburdened agencies are only able to file lawsuits on behalf of a tiny percentage of complainants.

Change Must First Come From Us

We can argue about sexual harassment into the next millennium (and no doubt we will). Yet no matter how we might define it, or who we might blame for it, there will be little improvement until we change the workplace into a professional environment that respects everyone. This will only come through a combination of individual effort and corporate action. Real change is possible only when the attitudes of men and women reflect the realities, not the myths, of working together.

These are very big challenges, and yet, let's be honest with ourselves. Ideas about whose fault it is or why men and women act the way they do, or who is going to fix this problem rarely makes much difference to the single mother who needs her job and finds herself receiving unwanted caresses at work by a senior level manager.

Nor does it offer much solace to the policewoman who is the object of repeated sexual hazing by her fellow officers. The fact that more women are gaining access to high-level positions doesn't change life for the bank vice-president who puts up with daily continual snipes about being promoted because of her looks.

17

We Must Work Together

The attitudes that lead to sexual harassment won't change overnight. Turning the workplace into a battlefield or avoiding each other is not the solution, either. We must work together.

Mandating behavior through corporate policy alone just doesn't work, and legal remedies are something few of us are willing to use. I believe passionately that the solution must come from **individual responsibility**. Each of us must recognize that we have a choice in how we treat one another and how we allow ourselves to be treated.

MYTHS AT WORK
*Generalizations, Stereotypes & Other
Oversimplifications about Sexual Harassment*

It only happens to weak women.
It only happens to young, pretty women.
It only happens in big companies.
It only happens to lower-level employees.

Women secretly welcome the attention.
Women bring it on themselves by acting sexy.
Women can't control themselves around men.

Men can't control themselves around women.
Men have a stronger sex drive than women.
Men and women need sex to be creative.

It isn't harassment if there's no touching.
It isn't a problem if you're aggressive with men.
It isn't a problem if you don't hire women.
It's impossible to prove.

Chapter 3

SEX, POWER, OR CROSSED SIGNALS?

Meredith and Jack

What motivates someone to engage in harassing behavior? Is he after sex? Is he trying to use his power to intimidate you? Or does he simply misunderstand that what he thinks is fun or harmless is something you don't like at all? Does he care?

It's no surprise that when I've asked men and women these questions about sexual harassment, they see it differently. Most women feel the issue is power. Most men say the motive is sex. And this difference in perception can create painful misunderstandings. In fact, the differences in how men and women perceive things about each other is exactly what's wrong most of the time. Consider the story of Meredith and Jack:

Meredith has worked for the past year as a telemarketing representative at a large company. She's enjoyed working for Jack, her immediate supervisor. They are both outgoing, friendly people. Jack likes to tease Meredith about her clothes and figure, and often makes comments to her such as, "If only the people on the other end of the phone could see you, Meredith, you'd break every sales record in this company!" Meredith enjoys this teasing, and she usually returns it, even though she isn't sexually attracted to Jack and

19

doesn't want to start a personal relationship with him.

As far is Jack is concerned, Meredith is "consenting" to a sexual flirtation. He does find her attractive. So he ups the ante, so to speak, and his comments now take on a more personal tone. "Every time you wear that dress, it gets my heart pumping, and I'd really like to show you the kind of rhythm it's making..."

These more explicit comments make Meredith uncomfortable. She thinks Jack is *coming on* to her, and she doesn't like it. She'd like to tell him that she doesn't want him to speak to her in this way, but she doesn't know how to tell him. How can she say anything to him without jeopardizing her job or making an enemy out of her boss?

Meredith is thinking of the risks involved in this situation. If she tells him to stop, will he make life miserable for her at work? Will he feel rejected, and resent her? Will he keep her from getting a promotion? Is he trying to use his position to get sexual favors from her? Does he really want to date her, or is he just trying to get a reaction from her? The tensions between them strain their work relationship.

Jack senses the change in Meredith, and he's confused. He can see she's acting differently, but he thinks she's being uptight for no good reason. He doesn't see any real difference between what he's saying now and what he said to her earlier. He's never touched her, and he has no indication from her that his comments upset her. If she told him they upset her, he'd be very surprised, but he would probably stop.

Jack is unaware that his power to promote, fire or affect the work environment for his employees, enters into the dynamic of this situation. In fact, most men rarely realize how the power difference in their roles could paralyze someone—and especially a woman—from speaking up to a superior. Jack doesn't think he's being intimidating to Meredith. To him, this is simply chemistry. It makes work more enjoyable. It's all part of the game.

Is this sexual coercion or a harmless flirtation? Meredith and Jack each see it differently.

The Male Perception: All in Fun?

Like Jack, most men who are in a position of power at work are so used to it that they take their power for granted. They see the sexual behavior as a man/woman interaction, instead of as a boss/worker relationship. It's often difficult for them to sense how coercive and threatening their power can be, especially when they believe that the "chase" or sexual game is in the spirit of good-natured fun.

For men who think this way, sexually-oriented behavior is a form of general, impersonal communication; the inevitable result of men and women being in close contact and naturally attracted to each other.

The Female Perception: A Personal Threat?

Meredith sees it from another perspective. Women usually view sexually-oriented behavior in a very personal and specific way. We almost always connect it to relationships, and are often keenly aware of our role in the relationship. Most of us have also been socialized to

21

be alert for any possible threat to our bodies, and we respond to unsolicited and unwanted attention by searching for signs of threat or potential coercion. Men are not likely to connect flirtation and seductive behavior with rape. Women, on the other hand, feel the line can be quickly and dangerously crossed.

The Work Environment Makes a Difference

This sensitivity to power relationships is especially true in the work environment, where women have generally held subordinate positions to men. A woman sitting in a public bar might have no problem at all in telling an obnoxious guy to leave her alone; but if they are at work and if he is her boss, things become much more complex. Her conditioning may have taught her that it's risky—or wrong—to stand up to a man who wields power over her. Her career survival instincts may tell her she's inviting disaster if she refuses or reports him.

The Path to Harassment

If Meredith never actually says anything to Jack about his behavior, can he legally be accused of sexual harassment? It depends. Whether the situation between Jack and Meredith constitutes a legal case of sexual harassment can differ from state to state. The inconsistency in laws, as well as inconsistencies in interpreting behavior and intent by attorneys, judges, and arbitrators adds to the confusion. Interpretations by the media, when reporting court cases and trends in the laws on sexual harassment, often confuse things even further.

For this reason, it's even more important for a woman to speak up and make it clear to her harasser that the behavior is unwelcome. Until the laws are clearer, and interpretations more consistent, women like Meredith will continue to bear an unfair burden of policing the workforce of offensive behavior. Speaking up may be difficult, but saying nothing can have other consequences, not the least of which is a possible negative impact on your case if you later decide to take legal action against your harasser. *(For a more detailed discussion of the laws on sexual harassment, turn to page 3.)*

More Crossed Signals

Fortunately, most men will stop harassing you if you make it clear that you don't welcome their behavior or attentions. Research shows that men often misread a woman's friendliness and see it as sexual interest. Because of this, they often don't realize that many women are insulted when men make sexual overtures in a workplace environment.

According to Dr. Barbara Gutek, who researched this topic extensively, few women see the workplace as the place to "...validate their sexual desirability... perhaps because they understand that they are too readily seen as potential sexual partners by men at work, and are too reluctantly seen as serious employees."[1]

---

1. Gutek, Barbara. *Sex and the Workplace: The Impact of Sexual Harassment on Women, Men and Organizations.* San Francisco: Jossey-Bass, 1985.

23

Many problems arise simply because men and women perceive behavior from such different perspectives. Some men who harass truly believe their behavior is innocent or harmless. Others have a far more serious intent. And sometimes, something that starts out relatively innocuous may turn into something else that makes us very uncomfortable.

Next, we'll look at different types of harassing behaviors and in the following section I'll show you how you can defend yourself against them.

What Women Think About Sexual Harassment

"It's all about power and control. Men know they can control women through sex. They always have and they always will."

"Men think they own the world and we are all put here to serve them. They think they can do anything they want and they usually get away with it."

"I don't think sex is the real issue. Mostly I think men try to see how they can get to women by making fun of them or making them feel self-conscious. Sexual harassment is a kind of put-down."

"When a man makes a sexual comment to me, I never think he's trying to have sex with me. I think, this guy's trying to throw me off balance or get control over me, to gain an advantage in some way."

"It's because women send the wrong messages. They flirt around and wear sexy clothes and then they expect men to treat them like nuns at work. Men just don't know how to deal with that, so things get out of hand."

"Women don't stand up for themselves. If a guy makes a pass at them, they just take it, or pretend it never happened, or else they end up quitting their jobs. No one I know would ever go to court over this… it's just not worth it. Most of my friends would rather just quit and work somewhere else."

What Men Think About Sexual Harassment

"Women say they want to be treated equally, but then they turn around and use their sexuality to compete against men. No man would ever do that."

"If women don't like it, they have a funny way of showing it. Most of the women I know love getting compliments. They expect you to say something. And they can dish out the dirt the same as any guy."

"It's a natural thing for men and women to flirt with each other. That's how it's supposed to be. Women can't stop being women and men can't stop being men."

"Whenever I see a woman dressed like a hooker at the office, I wonder what they're talking about when they accuse men of harassment. They should look in the mirror and ask themselves honestly what message they're sending."

Chapter 4

FOUR TYPES OF HARASSING BEHAVIOR

The Misfit, the Casanova, the Braggart, and the Intimidator

U nderstanding why individuals act in a certain way can be very empowering to you—it can give you insights into what's behind their words or actions so that they become less threatening to you. It can also prepare you to be more effective in dealing with their negative behavior.

The Misfit

Socially inept behavior, expressed by the Misfit, is characterized by a harasser who feels awkward around women, and who often can only relate to them as sex objects. He just doesn't know how to behave correctly in the work environment, or for that matter socially. He may actually be very insecure and physically uncomfortable around women.

The Misfit may use crude or sexually offensive language. This harasser may be infatuated by you, but can't begin or maintain a conversation. He is clumsy or insensitive to your reactions. This might lead him to use words like *honey, sweetheart, lover* that seem perfectly acceptable to him, but are out of place at work.

This is the guy who stands too close, hovers around your desk, bumps into you "accidentally" at the water fountain. Even though his behavior may make you highly uncomfortable, he often gets away with it because you might tend to dismiss him as one who doesn't know any better.

Debbie's Story
Age 30, Receptionist

I work as a receptionist for a law firm downtown. What I went through involved a client. This guy was awful, I mean the worst. He came into the office and told the most rank stories you can imagine, and he always leaned over the desk and leered down my front or made stupid, disgusting sounds like heavy breathing or sucking noises that just made me sick. I thought he was a complete jerk and I hated to see him come through the office door.

I told one of the attorneys and he told me to put up with it because this guy was one of our biggest clients and brought in more money to the firm in a year than what my salary was. Another of the attorneys told me I'd better not make the client get upset or anything because they could get a new receptionist in a minute.

The Casanova

Casanova behavior is characterized by a harasser who believes that any woman's problems, personal or otherwise, come down to one thing: her need for sex. He defines women in terms of how sexually fulfilled he thinks they are. He's the type who will say, "You're just upset because you aren't getting any," or make similar comments when you reject his advances or complain about his behavior.

The Casanova normally isn't selective. He'll usually pick on any woman he can find as a target. He thinks that romancing women is his calling, and he's the flirt, the tease, the seducer. He believes women like it—and in fact, function better—if they are reminded of their sexuality and his. And for him, sex is never inappropriate, regardless of the environment or situation.

Women often don't know whether to be annoyed or flattered by the attentions of a Casanova, especially those we might call "smooth operators." That's why we often find ourselves confused about his motivations or hestitant to say anything to him about his behavior.

Dee Dee's Story
Age 25, Administrative Assistant

I was the newest and youngest member of the department, so naturally, I expected to take a lot of flak. This one guy started coming on to me almost from the first day I was there. Most of the other women just rolled their eyes whenever he started flirting around, but I don't know, I kind of felt flattered. At least he seemed friendly, and I didn't think he meant anything by it.

Then he started leaving me little gifts on my desk. First it was a cupcake or doughnut from the break cart. Then it was a single red rose. Once he heard me talking about the new CD player I got, and the next day there was a this CD on my desk called "Music to Make Love By."

I kept telling myself he was just being friendly, or maybe he was just a natural born

29

flirt. But then he started leaving these sex things... a pair of thong bikini underpants, and then some XXX-rated postcards. Those things were horrible. They embarassed me. I didn't know what to say to him, and I was afraid the others would find out what he was doing, and think it was my fault.

The Braggart

This behavior is characterized by a harasser who believes that all women should be tolerated as sex objects. He acts condescendingly toward women, and may find it difficult to work with them, even if he has a female boss. He frequently boasts about the "hard line" he takes with women, to "keep them in line." He's the harasser who tries to build up his own masculinity at women's expense, and he's usually trying to impress other men with his "macho" attitude toward women.

The Braggart also makes belittling comments such as "That's just like a woman..., " or attempts to relate everything you do to the fact that you're a female. He may spread sexual rumors about you to his male counterparts and often infers to others that he knows something about you sexually.

Brianne's Story
Age 29, Marketing Service Representative

Every year the company has a big display booth at the food show in New York. It's a big deal, and everybody wants to go because it's really a blast. Last year I got to go and I was really excited until we got there and I found out that all the men had to wear tuxedos and the women were given these sequined little bikini things that were little more than bras and G-strings. I couldn't believe it. I have a college degree and I work in the marketing department, I just couldn't believe they expected me to do this. When I spoke to my boss about it, he told me that the company's display was rated tops in the industry, and this was the kind of promo that got people to stop by the booth. He told me that I should be flattered, because no one got asked to go on the trip unless they had a great body. I asked him if that's how they chose the men to go, and he just looked at me like I was crazy or something. He really thought I was nuts to be so upset over it, and I don't think he ever figured it out.

No matter what type of harassing behavior you encounter, most men will stop such behavior when you tell them clearly that you're not interested or find their behavior objectionable. The harassment may not be intended to intimidate you. In fact, the Braggart may be shocked to discover that you think of his behavior as sexual harassment.

You may believe that most harassers won't stop just because you ask them, but you'd be surprised. According to a recent survey of readers sponsored by *Working Woman* magazine, over 90% of the unwelcome sexual remarks were never repeated once the woman spoke up and asked them to stop.

Consider Barbara's story:

Barbara's Story
Age 28, Assembly Line Worker

I really hated the stupid remarks and catcalls I kept getting from this group of guys leaving from the night crew when I came on shift. This one guy in particular just wouldn't let up. He kept making lewd gestures with his hips and asking me if I was going to be next month's Playmate. It was really just childish, stupid stuff, but it kinda got to me, you know? I dreaded that walk from the parking lot.

Then one day, I just turned to that guy and told him in no uncertain terms to knock it off, that I really hated what he was doing and the things they were saying to me. I just wasn't going to put up with him anymore. He absolutely went silent and looked at me like I'd fired a gun or something.

I really don't think he had a clue that I didn't like all those remarks—he just kinda got carried away with his little game. After that day, he never said another word to me except, "Hi." And he must have told the others to lay off too, because really, they all sort of lightened up and quit giving me grief.

Sometimes it may take a little more to make a harasser come around, but it can be done. This is Randall's story:

Randall's Story
Age 38, Office Manager

I just went along with the teasing and joking in the office and it seemed like the women liked it. I liked it. It made it sort of—exciting—to work there, you know? But it turned out that the women didn't like it as much as the guys thought. At first I was shocked and really mad that something like this investigation could cost me a promotion—it seemed so petty and stupid—we were just joking around with those women, having a good time. They called it sexual harassment. I was so mad.

Later I started thinking about their side of it—the women—and I realized that what we were doing was just dumb. We really liked those women and yet we were treating them like they weren't even human...just sex objects or something. The whole thing just got out of hand. I would never treat my wife or daughter like that, and I would hate it if somebody else did. I just came to the conclusion that what we'd been doing was really unfair and didn't really contribute anything to getting the job done. Believe me, I will never do anything like that again.

There are ways you can stand up to the Misfit, the Casanova, and the Braggart types of harassing behavior. Of course, you may have to say, "NO!" or "STOP!" a number of times to get your message across. You may also have to listen to excuses or even complaints about being misunderstood or misinterpreted. You may have to help the harasser understand

33

that it isn't your interpretation of the situation that's wrong, but the harassing behavior. In Section II, I'll tell you how, but first I'll describe the Intimidator.

The Intimidator

This type of behavior is characterized by harassers who have positions of power at work and use their power to sexually harass women. Fortunately there are relatively few of these men in the workplace, yet they are responsible for the majority of sexual harassment cases reported.

Often, this kind of harasser harbors a deeply-held distrust of women and may see them as intruders on man's traditional turf—the workplace. He may exhibit his distrust openly, or in much more subtle ways. He's likely to be highly competitive and to view women as challenging him personally. He may be on a personal mission to prove that women are inferior and don't have the ability to stick it out.

He may use sexual harassment to "put you in your place" and show you that you're only a sex object to him, rather than a skilled employee or a contributing team member or co-worker.

The majority of sexual harassment cases involve boss/subordinate relationships. The relationship between the Intimidator and his victim is often based on a complex web of dependency and dominance that's common in many organizational power structures.

In some cases, however, the Intimidator may be a co-worker. Often his perceived power may only be in his imagination or yours! Either way, he'll try to prove to you that he has the power to intimidate or humiliate you at work. He'll do this by demanding sex or using other forms of sexual harassment, such as lewd gestures, profanity, or offensive remarks.

The Intimidator often betrays the trust placed in him. Some women are highly susceptible to a betrayal of trust, because they often put a lot of faith into the strong interpersonal relationships they develop at work.

We may look to men to offer direction and teach us about leadership and power. We may seek validation of our own worth from men whom we consider to have "made it." Very often these men are our immediate supervisors or other authority figures within the organization. This intrinsic trust can makes us extremely vulnerable. We are more vulnerable when part of our investment in these relationships comes from insecurities about ourselves, and/or an ambiguity about power and position. An Intimidator who is aware of this can switch suddenly from a warm, interested confidant to a harasser. One of the ways he does this most destructively is by demanding sex.

The impact of this betrayal can often be scarring. At first it may be shocking. Then anger, humiliation, fear, helplessness, resentment and even guilt may follow. Such a betrayal can leave a wound that remains throughout a working career. For those of us who have suffered abusive relationships in the past, this type of harassment can be especially painful.

Being betrayed by an Intimidator can make you feel that you're trapped in a situation with no escape. Paula's story is typical.

Paula's Story
Age 33, Aeronautical Engineer:

I was thrilled to get to go to Washington, D.C., for the firm's presentation to the Pentagon. I had worked on that project for over two years, and I was the only one out of our department selected to accompany the president and the other divisional chiefs. It was my big opportunity to prove myself, and I gave the performance of my life.

Afterwards, the president invited me to his hotel room to celebrate. I was happy to go, and why wouldn't I be? I was on top of the world, and I assumed he'd invited everybody on the team. When I got to his room, he invited me in, and poured some champagne, and told me how well I had done. I was glad to hear it. Then he put his hand on me. Here I was with one of the most powerful men in the entire industry, in a hotel room with no witnesses, and this guy was making a pass at me!

I broke away from him and started crying. He stopped trying to kiss me, but he sat me down and tried to "reason" with me. He told me I was being foolish, that he could really help me get ahead and I could work on anything I wanted. He stroked my hair and let me know that if I went along with him, I could expect lots of perks. He told me it would be the best decision I'd ever made if I became his "friend."

I just couldn't stop sobbing. It was like my whole world just crumbled around me. I couldn't believe it was happening to me, and I had never even seen it coming. I felt stupid, and just devastated, and I also felt this terrible rage at the injustice of it all. Finally, when I was able to calm down, I told him I'd never do anything like he suggested. I told him to leave me alone and to never come near me again.

That's when his whole attitude changed. He told me I could forget about a career with the company; that there were plenty of others who would gladly take my place on the "winning team." He told me I was throwing away my future and being a fool.

Sure enough, he was true to his word. When I went back to work, it was like I went back to Siberia. I sat in my office with absolutely nothing to do. No projects, no meetings, nothing. I was completely out of the loop, totally ostracized. I tried to talk to somebody about it, but nobody wanted to be seen talking to me in my office or even in the halls. He'd put the word out on me, and they made me feel like a leper. He was the president of the company. Who was going to believe me?

I finally quit my job, but I went to the state Human Rights Commission and filed a grievance against the company. They ended up settling with me for over $325,000. As far as I know, the president is still there.

When you're facing an Intimidator, all too often you find yourself caught in a web of indecision and self- doubt. You know that very often, the Intimidator *does* have the power to affect your work situation. He's aware of the risks you face in confronting him and knows that the inequity of your positions may make your credibility an issue with others. How many women have felt that their lower status in the company makes them and their version of events less credible than the boss who is harassing them?

Don't fall into this negative thinking trap. There are ways to confront, and effectively respond to the Intimidator. In the next section, I'll show you how you can resist this kind of intimidation. It's a very powerful advantage for you to have.

Traits of a Typical Harasser

- Very alert to physical appearances
- Uses sexual gestures or innuendoes in conversation
- Tells jokes or stories with sexual orientations
- Uses sexually-oriented slang or profanity
- Describes people, situations and activities in sexual terms
- Brags about sex and sexual activities
- Brings sexually-oriented materials into the workplace
- Acts uninformed or confused about sexual harassment

Traits of the Typical Intimidator

- Displays negative attitudes toward women
- Resents the intrusion of women in the workplace
- Displays anger toward women
- Views women in the traditional roles: wife, mother, sex object
- Avoids genuine friendships with women
- Exaggerates his own importance and authority
- Hides lack of self-esteem by an overbearing or arrogant attitude
- Becomes extremely defensive or highly confrontational, especially with women
- Displays prejudices against women
- Uses sexist or racist analogies and anecdotes in conversation
- Focuses attention on inadequacies of women
- Devalues contributions of women
- Uses threats and bullying tactics with women subordinates
- Assigns women work of lesser importance
- Positions women in subordinate or support roles
- Insists on formality as a sign of respect from subordinates
- Directly or indirectly denies promotions to women
- Supports pay inequities between men and women

SECTION II

HOW TO SAY NO

Introduction

Saying NO to sexual harassment on the job ought to be easy, but it can be one of the hardest things any of us has to do. The chapters in this section will help you gain the skills and courage you need to confront your harasser assertively, and with confidence, so you can say NO and still feel good about yourself.

NOTE: *If at any time you suspect the harassment could escalate to the point of physically endangering you, please don't hesitate to report your fears immediately to someone at your company who can help you. No job or relationship is worth risking your personal safety.*

Chapter 5

SETTING LIMITS

Say YES to Self-Respect

Standing up for yourself doesn't have to mean becoming hostile or sacrificing your work relationships. Ignoring the situation or avoiding each other doesn't work either. As **9to5**, the National Association of Working Women points out in its harassment prevention guide, the way to combat sexual harassment is not by avoiding contact, but by practicing respect.

Communicating assertively doesn't mean being impolite. It means engaging in a balanced, honest exchange that benefits and respects both parties. If you're submitting to sexual harassment because you don't want to hurt your harasser's feelings or damage his ego, you are creating an uneven exchange for yourself. Experts in assertiveness training say that you'll be respected more, not less, when you confront situations honestly and directly.

Learning to project confidence—and demonstrating that you know how to take care of yourself and aren't afraid to do it—will make you a far less attractive candidate for harassment. Harassers are less likely to target you if you maintain a self-assured, business-like demeanor that commands respect.

Do You Suffer from 'Victim Thinking' ?

Some of us unknowingly send out signals that let others know they won't get much opposition from us, regardless of how they treat us. Some of us play along with behavior that makes us uncomfortable, because we're afraid that we'll alienate others if we don't. And some of us feel it's useless to say anything, because we believe nothing will change.

These signals reflect what I call 'victim thinking'. It's a frame of mind that causes us to feel powerless to challenge the negative behavior that's robbing us of self-respect. Victim thinking exaggerates our fear that if we stand up to a harasser, we'll suffer consequences worse than the harassment.

Do You Blame Yourself ?

Our unwillingness to speak up is also reinforced by the 'Eve' myth that, as a woman, we are to blame for what's happened. Men often accuse us of flaunting our sexuality in the workplace, of not playing fair, or of deserving what we get. And they're not alone in that assessment. Many of the women I've interviewed over the years also assign blame to the woman involved in sexual harassment. And yet studies show that women are rarely flattered by being propositioned sexually at work, regardless of the situation.

I don't agree with people who blame the victim. I don't think women "ask for it." I certainly don't believe that harassment is a natural consequence of working with men. Even if a woman acts or dresses in a way her harasser finds arousing or provocative, he is responsible for his behavior.

44

Sexual harassment is not a reaction, but an action consciously chosen. 'Victim thinking' perpetuates the cycle of abuse. You can break that cycle, and show yourself ultimate respect. Refuse to accept the blame for abusive behavior directed at you.

What's Your Workplace Image?

What you are responsible for is the image you project. Whether you're the head of the company, or a trainee, if you're dissatisfied with your image, you can change it. Your goal, of course, is to cultivate the kind of presence that lets others know you're a person they should respect.

You can do this without going against the system, or setting yourself apart in any way. Simply pay attention to how you present yourself at work. Learning to speak up begins with feeling good about yourself. Here are some key areas to consider:

Dress the Part

Forget the fashion magazines that show executive women wearing provocative office attire. It doesn't take much fashion savvy to figure out that this kind of clothing sends a message that's hard to ignore.

Men in general are sensitive to physical appearances, and they often react sexually to sensory signals. Even if you feel capable of fending off unwelcome advances, you'd be wise to consider carefully the signals you may be sending, especially if you want to be taken seriously. According to Professor Barbara Gutek, most men cannot simultaneously see a woman as a sex object and a skilled businesswomen. They can typically perceive of men as both, but not women.

Your Body Talks Too

- The way you carry yourself, and the way you move, says a lot about you.

- A negative body image may signal the harasser that you're easy prey.

- Some women are oblivious of the signal their body language sends.

If you're uncomfortable with your body, consider taking a class on body image, movement expression or learning one of the martial arts. These activities can help you gain and project confidence.

What You Say Tells a Lot About You

You may believe that using locker-room language will make you sound tough and help you fit in better with the men at work. This is questionable. Some men are very aroused when they hear women use profanity, even if they frequently hear that kind of language from men. The use of profanity may send others a message you don't intend to give them.

Think Twice Before You Flirt or Touch Someone

It's natural to sometimes feel an attraction for someone at work, but if you indulge in flirting, ask for a hug, or touch someone in a friendly way, your gesture can be misinterpreted. Studies show that men tend to misread friendly gestures as signs that women are interested in them sexually.[1]

Rules to Live By

You have more ability than you think to influence the way others treat you. Making conscious choices about your own behavior, instead of only reacting to others, helps you feel good about yourself. It gets you out of the trap of 'victim thinking'.

Here are some guidelines which can help you base your working code of conduct on respect for yourself and those you work with every day. These are not an arbitrary set of rules, but a framework for what I call *the new workplace protocol*. It's a protocol for both men and women.

The New Workplace Protocol

- Be consistent and treat others consistently.

- Don't barter sexuality for popularity or advancement.

- Dress appropriately for your job without drawing attention to your sexuality.

- Don't use "body language" that others may interpret as sexual.

- Keep personal relationships separate from work relationships.

---

1. Gutek, Barbara. *Sex and the Workplace: The Impact of Sexual Behavior and Harassment on Women, Men and Organizations.* San Francisco: Jossey-Bass, 1985.

Chapter 6

WHAT ABOUT ROMANCE?

How It Can Affect You in the Workplace

So what about romance? Do all of these cautions about sex and power mean we are going to declare the workplace off-limits for courtship?

Not likely. Work is the number one place where we meet the people who become our companions, our friends, our lovers and our spouses. It's totally unrealistic to expect that romance won't happen when men and women work together. It's also unrealistic to think a company policy against dating co-workers is going to change anything.

Virtually every self-help book or contemporary magazine contains an article about the pitfalls of dating your boss. Career guides caution you about having an affair with a co-worker, the need to keep your business life separate from your personal life, and the dangers of allowing your heart to interfere with your judgment. It's very sound advice. The only problem is, it just doesn't work for most of us. When you are smitten, you scarcely heed advice like this. We just don't see clearly when we are in love.

Good Love Gone Bad

The problem with on-the-job liaisons, of course, is that there's always the possibility that the intimacy of a romantic relationship could lead to misunderstandings or even abuse. When the lovers hold different level positions at work, or when one supervises the other, it can cause problems both on and off the job. Love gone wrong can turn into retaliation and sometimes harassment when one of the lovers can't accept that it's over, and tries to use the work relationship to "get even."

There's also the problem of co-workers. Others might feel you're taking unfair advantage of your special position with the boss, and that they're losing out. When other workers feel their job or the working environment is being negatively affected by a liaison going on in the office, it can cause morale problems, as well as what's called third-party harassment. It's a form of discrimination that's illegal in most states.

You could also find that you're the focus of unfair treatment yourself—being denied a promotion for which you're qualified or a raise you feel you deserve—because your lover doesn't want to "show favoritism" toward you. These things do happen, and when they do, you can handle these situations better if you are prepared for them.

I join the chorus of advice givers who suggest it's probably not the best idea to have a romantic involvement with someone at work—especially someone who is your supervisor or boss. Career considerations aside, it's just hard to balance the personal with the professional relationship when they are so

49

closely aligned. However, having done my duty and said that, here's my short list of things to at least consider if you find yourself in this situation:

Keep it discreet

Many people have a special radar that senses the romantic electricity between two co-workers. If you're sending megawatt signals, you can be sure someone other than your 'intended' is picking them up. This might lead someone else to think you would welcome any sexual overture.

Avoid Gossip and Gossiping

Office gossip is a tempting subject when you work together, but some insider information is too hot to handle. Talking about your love relationship with others at work, or talking to your lover about others at work, can cause fellow employees to mistrust you, or your motives.

Make Your Own Career

Many people continue to believe that women can only make it to the top of the career ladder by "sleeping" their way there. It's really a hard charge to fight if you're having an affair that's common knowledge in the office. If you can't avoid the gossip, at least don't make your lover your career advisor. You'll feel a lot better about your achievements and choices if they're your own.

Patti's Story
Age 28, Claims Adjuster

Bart and I had been dating for almost seven months when they announced an opening for a senior claims adjuster in the new Chicago office. My family was in Chicago, and I'd wanted to move closer to home for years. I was absolutely qualified for that job, and I just couldn't wait to apply.

As it turned out, Bart was the one who got to decide who would be transferred. The fact that we were dating shouldn't have had anything to do with my being promoted, but of course, it became the main issue. Everyone in the office just assumed he'd give me the transfer, and some of the other adjusters weren't too kind about their opinion of that deal.

Bart and I both struggled with it, but in the end, he gave the promotion to someone else. He said he just couldn't risk having people think he was using his personal relationship to influence his business decisions. So I didn't move to Chicago.

Chapter 7

SENDING CLEAR SIGNALS

Learning How to Communicate

There's a conspiracy of silence that surrounds and perpetuates sexual harassment in the workplace. You refuse to be part of this of conspiracy when you assertively respond to your harasser. Actively responding may take courage, but it's easier to do when you know what to say and when to say it. At the very least, speaking up for yourself is healthier than seething in silence. More often than not, your assertiveness will stop the harasser in his tracks.

In this chapter, you'll learn some general principles for formulating assertive responses. Later chapters will offer different types of assertive responses you can use with a harasser. You'll learn how to assert yourself in a way that gets your message across, but which can also allow you to maintain a working relationship with the harasser.

Phrasing your initial response so that it allows the person who has offended you to "save face" is to your advantage. A man who feels humiliated or rejected may retaliate in subtle, or not so subtle, ways that make working with him difficult. That could pose a threat to your own career.

Be careful not to confuse assertiveness with aggression. Aggressive behavior is confrontational and often threatening. It rarely encourages or improves communication. Being assertive means being honest, direct and specific about what you like or dislike. It means refusing to back down when you know you are right—even if the other person becomes angry or tries to intimidate you. It also means responding in a way that's appropriate to the situation.

The Benefits of Speaking Up

If you aren't in the habit of asserting yourself, it can feel scary at first. But take heart. It gets easier each time you do it. You can begin to prepare yourself by practicing with friends, or by spending five or ten minutes a day visualizing yourself being assertive. You can do this on the way to work. Gaining the courage to assert yourself is well worth whatever effort it takes.

Asserting yourself is a terrific confidence builder. Others will experience you as a powerful person. You'll become better able to take care of yourself in situations when someone tries to intimidate or embarrass you. Best of all, you're likely to get the offensive behavior to stop.

Acting assertively places the responsibility for negative behavior back on the harasser. It shows him that you neither invited nor are willing to accept his unwelcome behavior. When you stand up to him, your harasser can no longer entertain his fantasy that you welcome such attention. If he's previously justified his harassing behavior by fantasizing your approval, he now has to face reality. Sometimes, this may be all it takes to get him to leave you alone.

The only time you should not speak up is if you feel the situation is dangerous. In this case, you should break off contact with your harasser immediately. *Don't risk your personal safety.*

How to Assert Yourself

How do you rebuff a harasser effectively? You start by being honest with yourself. If someone's off-color remarks or behavior make you angry, upset, frustrated or frightened, it may seem more natural for you to squash your feelings than to express them. But hiding your feelings does not let him know what you find objectionble and how you're affected by his behavior. Honor your feelings. You have a right to speak up about something that has made you uncomfortable. If you think the harassment line has been crossed, trust your instincts. If you're not sure, use the Four-Question Reality Check explained on page 5.

Tell the person who's offended you what it is specifically that you don't like. You don't need to over-react or become hostile, but you want to express yourself very directly and clearly. If you equivocate or sidestep the issue, chances are he'll do it again.

Each of the verbal rebuffs suggested in this and later chapters incorporate four basic principles. These simple rules will help you phrase an assertive response to your harasser.

Response Rule #1: Be Direct.

This is hard for most of us, but it's essential. If you're indirect or vague, you lose ground and your harasser gains it. If you don't say what you mean, you may lead him to believe that his behavior is okay with you. One of the primary excuses men give for repeating harassing behavior is *"I thought it was okay! She never said anything to me about not liking it!"*

Here's an example of such a situation. Compare the ineffective responses with the direct one that gets the point across.

SITUATION:
A co-worker keeps leaving you messages on your voice mail that are sexually suggestive.

Don't pretend you never got the message.

DON'T SAY:
"Some people could get in a lot of trouble around here if they don't learn to keep their mouths shut."

SAY:
"The messages you've been leaving me on the voice mail are inappropriate, and I don't like them. Please don't do it again."

Response Rule #2: Be Consistent

Sometimes you may have to repeat your message to make sure your harasser understands "NO." Because men are often used to being sexual initiators, they have learned over the years that 'no' doesn't always mean 'no.' They may expect a certain amount of coyness about sex from women, or they may think you don't mean what you said. Some men may need to hear you say "NO" several times clearly before they believe you.

You'll be more believable if you're consistent in your response. An inconsistent response can convey the opposite of what you actually mean, says Dr. Deborah

55

Tannen,[1] the popular linguistics specialist who's studied communication between the sexes.

Response Rule #3: Focus on the Real Problem

Some harassers are more persistent than others. A common tactic is to try to engage you in a debate about his intentions, or to embarrass you in a way that puts you on the defensive. Don't allow him to shift your focus from the real problem: *his unprofessional and offensive behavior.*

No matter what *he* says, *your* answer should be consistently the same. Once you've made your point directly and clearly, end the discussion. Tell him you've said what you've needed to say and you don't want to discuss it further.

Here's an example of a situation. Notice how the second response shifts the focus of the conversation back where it belongs—to the offensive behavior of the harasser.

SITUATION:
Your supervisor keeps making comments about your figure that suggest your appearance is the reason you're the top salesperson in the department. When you call him on it, he says you're being overly sensitive and tells you to "lighten up."

SAY:
"When you make comments about my body, it's upsetting to me. It makes me feel that you don't value the skill I bring

---

1. Tannen, Deborah. *You Just Don't Understand: Women and Men In Conversation.* New York: Random House, 1990.

to this sales team. I hear it as a put-down and I don't like it. Please don't say such things to me again."

DON'T SAY:

"That's not fair. I can't help the way I'm built, and I'm not being sensitive!" or DON'T SAY: "I wish you'd stop saying that stuff about me."

Response Rule #4: Trust Your Instincts

If a situation becomes sexually charged, and it makes you uncomfortable, don't hesitate to follow your instincts. The following scenario demonstrates how responding indecisively can escalate the problem.

HE SAYS:

"That was a great presentation! What you need is a reward..."

SHE SAYS:
"Well... I... uh..."

HE SAYS:
"Why don't we start with a big hug (he reaches for her...)

SHE SAYS:
"Hey, don't do that... what if somebody saw us?"

HE SAYS:
"Close the door, baby, and they won't see a thing."

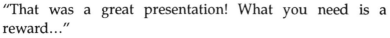

Here's a much better, more assertive way to handle that same situation:

HE SAYS:
"That was a great presentation! What you need is a reward… "

SHE SAYS:
(stepping back from him immediately when she senses a problem.) "We all did a good job."

HE SAYS:
"Yeah, but you were terrific! Why don't we start with a big hug." (He reaches for her.)

SHE SAYS:
(moving to the door) "Please don't hug me. Perhaps you don't realize how uncomfortable that makes me."

HE SAYS:
"Hey, I didn't mean anything by it! Jeez, don't get all upset."

SHE SAYS:
"I'm not upset. I just prefer to keep our relationship professional. Thanks for understanding."

It's wise to anticipate how you might respond to a situation like this, because it's a common one faced by many of us. *Pay particular attention to the simplicity of the assertive response.* It's direct, honest, and it's also courteous. Something as simple as thanking him for understanding your position makes your request conciliatory rather than confrontational. An encounter like this might make both of you feel a bit awkward initially, but chances are good that both of you will be able to put the incident behind you with no hard feelings.

Tips on Timing

When should you speak up? In general, a timely response is best. In most situations, the longer you delay, the more likely the situation will deteriorate.

There are some situations, however, where it may not be to your best advantage to confront your harasser immediately. What if he has a habit of joking about your body in front of others in a meeting? What if those people are his superiors or important clients?

Saying something to him right then, even though you might be right in doing so, could have some negative repercussions for you. Given the prevailing attitudes toward women in many work environments, you might find yourself the object of criticism because you spoke up and embarrassed him in front of other men. This could ultimately hurt your own career.

The politics of the situation may dictate that you wait until after the meeting to confront your harasser. Let him know that you delayed speaking to him to save both of you from embarrassment, and that you will not hesitate to speak up if he does it again. Here's how you might handle a situation like this:

Start by saying:
"Frank, I want to speak to you privately about something that is very upsetting to me. Can we talk now, or would you like to schedule an appointment for later this morning?"

This approach shows that you're being direct, stating your concerns, and proposing a specific time to talk. By specifically asking for a time to meet (rather than vaguely asking, "Can we talk sometime?"), you are

59

giving him some maneuvering room. You're also making it clear that you do not want to delay your talk until next week. If he does put you off, and you can't convince him you need to talk about it right away, you might want to consider beginning a journal to document any subsequent incidents.

If he is open to listening, say:
"This morning in the meeting with the area managers, you made a comment about my figure. That comment was very embarrassing to me, and I'm sure you agree with me that it had nothing to do with the X3-11 project."

Specify what happened and what you found offensive. By pointing out how the behavior was unrelated to the job, you remind him that you expect professional behavior from him without appearing to give him a lecture. You've also told him in a gentle way. Beginning a sentence with "I am sure you agree with me," is more conciliatory, less confrontational.

Next say:
"I didn't say anything to you in the meeting because I wanted to tell you how I feel about it without bringing it up in front of the other managers. However, If you do choose to embarrass me like that again, I won't be so considerate.

This shows him that you are professional enough to consider his dignity and yours. Yet it doesn't allow him to think that you're going to ignore future remarks. You've set the tone for the professional business relationship you expect from him, and you've also let him know the consequences if he does it again. You've specifically asked him to stop his comments, and you've let him know how you feel about it.

This is assertive behavior. It's a positive approach to a negative situation. Both of you can walk away from this encounter with your dignity intact. You can respect him for complying with your request, and he can respect you for being assertive, and sensitive about timing your remarks. Isn't this better than seething in silence and letting your anger impair your ability to work together?

Body Signals: Ways to Reinforce Your Message

In this chapter, you've learned some of the basics of asserting yourself. The next three chapters provide you with many assertive responses which you can adapt to a variety of situations.

There are other skills that can add emphasis to your response. You'll come across even more forcefully if you use your tone of voice and body language to reinforce your words. In her popular book, *You Just Don't Understand: Women and Men In Conversation*, Dr. Deborah Tannen makes the point that words alone may be misleading, but tone of voice rarely is.[2]

Experiment with inflection and tone as you read aloud the responses in the upcoming chapters. Practicing them with a friend will give you the opportunity

---

2. Tannen, Beborah. *You Just Don't Understand: Women and Men in a Conversation*. New York: Random House, 1990.

to critique each other's delivery and to exchange ideas. You can also speak into a tape recorder to hear how you sound. You should aim for a calm, confident delivery that lets your harasser know that you mean what you say. Keep trying until you feel comfortable with your delivery.

A little preparation in advance will make it easier for you to assert yourself. If you find it difficult to control your emotions, lower your voice and speak more slowly than normal. Take a few deep breaths before you speak. That will help you retain control.

Body language can also convey assertiveness or passivity. When someone is treating you inappropriately, you may feel embarrassed and humiliated. It can take a supreme effort not to look down, look away or act submissive. However, these are passive signals that confirm victim behavior, and they could give your harasser the green light to continue. If you want to appear assertive, follow these five suggestions:

1. **Maintain eye contact with the person.**

   Look directly at your harasser when you are speaking to him. Let your eyes convey your disapproval openly and directly.

2. **Step back or away from the person.**

   A small step backwards shows you want to break off contact. It also puts distance between you and the person whose behavior you find objectionable. Dr. Deborah Tannen notes that the amount of space between two speakers often sends signals about their relationship. When you are in a group, you can let others know you choose to disengage from this person by just stepping back.

3. **Don't smile**.

   Smiling while you are saying "no" sends a mixed message. Don't detract from the seriousness of what you're saying by smiling or treating it like a joke. If you are not amused by what was said or done, don't make light of it.

4. **Walk away from the person**.

   Walking away sends a clear message that you find a conversation or situation unacceptable. If this is the best way to take care of yourself in the situation, don't worry about being polite.

5. **Don't make threatening gestures**.

   Making your hands into fists, pointing your finger or pencil at someone, crossing your arms in front of you, or placing your hands on your hips can be threatening and provoking to some harassers. Try to assume a more relaxed, alert posture that reflects self-confidence and awareness.

63

Chapter 8

THE THREE LEVELS OF SAYING NO

This chapter will help you develop effective verbal and physical skills in confronting your harasser.

The more prepared you are—knowing exactly what you're going to say, and how you will say it—will help you in controlling your situation and stopping your harasser.

You'll be guided through three levels of verbal responses—the GENTLE REBUFF, the STRONGER REBUFF, and the FINAL REBUFF. This chapter also will describe helpful physical techniques that are appropriate to each level of response.

Learning how to respond when someone says or does something you find objectionable is vital to maintaining your dignity.

The rebuffs are designed to allow your harasser to step back, and with dignity too. It shows respect for the working relationship, while showing you're not being intimidated by behavior you find objectionable.

LEVEL ONE: The Gentle Rebuff

The gentle rebuff is a reasonable response to behavior you personally find unreasonable. It allows you to assert yourself and still take the other person's feelings into account.

This category of response is appropriate the first or second time you respond to someone who has spoken to you, or behaved toward you in a way that you find objectionable. You can afford to be gracious at this level, and give him an opportunity to stop the behavior without losing face. Graciousness, on your part, will allow the two of you to keep working together without continually sniping at each other or doing damage to both of your careers.

You'll find numerous examples of this style of response below. Read them over carefully, as if you were "learning your lines." Choose the responses that suit your own personal style, and adapt the words so they're your own. Just be sure to keep them in the same spirit. You may feel silly practicing them now, but practicing your response is good insurance against being caught off-guard by a situation without an effective response.

Your ACTION PLAN for the Gentle Rebuff

Guidelines

Ask your harasser politely but clearly to stop the unwanted behavior. Don't offend him or bruise his ego.

Action Plan

- Familiarize yourself with the level-one verbal responses.
- Complete the Four-Question Reality Check.
- Be prepared to advance to the Stronger Rebuff, if necessary.

Level One Assertive Responses

Notice that the preferred response in each situation incorporates the principles you learned in the last chapter. To help you, I've paired each preferred response with a non-assertive response, so you can recognize the difference.

SITUATION:
He asks you for a date, or suggests he would like to "get to know you better."

YOUR RESPONSE:
Tell him you want to keep your relationship professional, not personal.

Telling him clearly that you do not welcome his advances is very important. It's much better than feigning interest, which isn't honest and may cause him to try harder to get you to say yes.

SAY:
Thanks, but I'm not interested in a personal relationship.

DON'T SAY:
Well, maybe another time (unless that's what you really intend).

SAY:
I like working with you, but I don't want to date you.

DON'T SAY:
Gee, I don't know, I'm really busy.

66

SAY:
I'm glad I'm assigned to this project with you, but I don't want to go out to dinner with you.

DON'T SAY:
I can't tonight, I'm too tired.

SAY:
I'm proud to be on your team here at work, but I don't want a personal relationship outside of work.

DON'T SAY:
I never date people from work. (Because you might change your mind some day.)

SAY:
I value and appreciate your opinions at work, but I don't want to mix business with my personal life.

DON'T SAY:
Aren't you married?!

SAY:
I really admire how professional you are, so I know you'll understand when I say I want our relationship to remain businesslike.

DON'T SAY:
What will everyone think?

SITUATION:
He makes a remark or gesture that makes you feel uncomfortable or threatened.

YOUR RESPONSE:
Tell him that you are disturbed by his behavior. Don't say that your husband, or boyfriend, or his wife, would be offended. That evasiveness makes you appear weak and indecisive and could lead the other person to conclude that his behavior is okay with you.

SAY:
Please do not say that to me. It offends me.

DON'T SAY:
My husband (boyfriend, father, co-workers, etc.) would be really upset if he heard you say that.

SAY:
Please stop doing that in front of me.

DON'T SAY:
What if someone else saw you?

SITUATION:
He hugs you or touches you in a personal way that you find invasive or offensive.

YOUR RESPONSE:
Tell him immediately that you don't want him to touch you.

Don't try to soften what you are saying, because he might misunderstand you and think it's okay to do it again.

SAY:
Please stop touching me. It makes me uncomfortable, and I don't like it.

DON'T SAY:
I don't think that's very nice.

SAY:
Please don't stand so close to me. It makes me uncomfortable.

DON'T SAY:
I hope people don't get the wrong impression from this.

SAY:
I don't want you to hug me again. It makes me uncomfortable.

DON'T SAY:
We could get in trouble for this...

SITUATION:
He makes a sexually-oriented comment to you that you don't like, such as "Has anyone ever told you you have really sexy legs?"

YOUR RESPONSE:
Question his intentions by linking them back to the job. Be very specific, and he'll get the message.

SAY:
How do my legs relate to this project? Your comment makes me feel very uncomfortable.

DON'T SAY:
Why would you say something like that?!

SAY:
What do my legs have to do with how I do my job?

DON'T SAY:
You wouldn't say that if you ever saw me in shorts...

SAY:
My legs have nothing to do with my work or job performance.

DON'T SAY:
Oh, I'll bet you say that to all the girls.

SITUATION:
He slips an offensive cartoon into your mail or leaves it on your desk and then makes sure you know it came from him.

YOUR RESPONSE:
Tell him exactly how you feel about it. Don't hide your feelings about it or try to be so polite that you obscure your meaning. And don't pretend you never saw it, because it will only encourage him to try it again.

SAY:
I don't like this. Please do not leave offensive things on my desk again.

DON'T SAY:
I wish you wouldn't do things like that.

SAY:
I really find that offensive and unprofessional.

DON'T SAY:
I don't think you should be doing something like this at work.

SAY:
This is my private work area. I want you to stop putting sexually offensive things like this on my desk.

DON'T SAY:
Gee, don't let anybody else around here see that...

SITUATION:
He says something you don't like, but you aren't sure what he meant by it. Ask him directly, so that you clearly understand him.

YOUR RESPONSE:
If you don't like his answer, don't hide your feelings, and don't apologize for feeling the way you do. Women often automatically respond to situations by saying "I'm sorry" when they are not to blame. Don't let him debate with you or put the blame on you either.

SAY:
NO, that is NOT okay with me.

DON'T SAY:
I hope you won't think I'm a prude, but...

SAY:
I want you to know I don't welcome that comment. Please stop saying these things to me.

DON'T SAY:
I'm sorry if I gave you the wrong impression, but...

SAY:
You're out of line with that comment. Please don't repeat it.

DON'T SAY:
You must think I'm weird or something...

SITUATION:
He teases you in a sexual or physical way and makes it appear as if you like being talked to in that way.

YOUR RESPONSE:
Be very specific in identifying the behavior as HIS responsibility. Harassers generally make assumptions about your complicity. Don't allow him to do that, even if you must interrupt him. Don't use the pronoun "we." Instead, speak for yourself and make it clear that he is speaking for himself.

SAY:
YOU are saying something I don't like at all.

DON'T SAY:
We shouldn't be saying things like this at work...

SAY:
YOU are making me very upset by saying that.

DON'T SAY:
We could really get in trouble for this...

SAY:
Please understand that I'm not interested. I don't like being spoken to that way.

DON'T SAY:
We shouldn't be having this conversation at work.

SAY:
You are mistaken if you believe I enjoy being spoken to like that. Please don't do it again.

DON'T SAY:
You'll regret saying something like that to me...

SITUATION:
He tells you a sexual joke that offends you.

YOUR RESPONSE:
Tell him to stop, or tell him you don't want to hear it, and then walk away. If he persists, try one of the following responses.

Be consistent in your position about sexual jokes. We often laugh at things we really don't think are funny to avoid hurting someone's feelings or to fit in with the group. This is especially true of sexual jokes, which often make both men and women feel uncomfortable in mixed company. Even if you enjoy such jokes some of the time, you're probably wiser to give your co-workers the impression that you don't want to hear them at work. For some men, telling sexual jokes is a kind of overture. Condoning or using sexual humor may indicate that you are receptive to someone's overtures.

NOTE: *If you decide to take this stance, make it consistent. Don't be afraid to interrupt someone as soon as you realize that a joke or story is sexually-oriented.*

SAY:
That's not funny to me.

SAY:
I don't like these sexual jokes.

DON'T SAY:
I've already heard that one and it's not all that funny...

SAY:
I have told you before that I don't like language like that; please stop repeating it.

DON'T SAY:
Why do you always say things like this around me?

Common Responses to Harassment You Should Avoid

Don't Trade Sexual Quips

Trying to verbally outmaneuver your harasser with sexual banter can make you appear as if you are enjoying the exchange. Most women find that this does little to actually stop the harassment. In fact, it may well cause it to escalate, since many men find this a kind of verbal foreplay that's provocative. If you don't intend to participate, then say so directly, without trying to be clever or by pretending you don't find it objectionable.

Don't De-value Yourself

Trying to deflect the harassment by devaluing yourself as a target sends a subtle message that you actually want attention, however negative. This kind of behavior gives your harasser a perfect opening to increase his efforts.

SAY:
NO, I am not interested.

DON'T SAY:
You wouldn't say that if you knew the real me…

SAY:
Please stop asking me to go out with you.

DON'T SAY:
You can find someone a lot better/younger/prettier (etc.) than me to date.

SAY:
Please stop saying that about me.

DON'T SAY:
I can't believe you'd say something like that to me.

Deny Wrong Assumptions About You

Directly countering a statement or innuendo with the truth makes it clear to your harasser that you refuse to take any responsibility for his behavior toward you. This can be particularly effective with harassers who may arrogantly assume that you would welcome any attention they offer you.

SAY:
You have no idea what my beliefs are. I want you to stop saying these things to me.

DON'T SAY:
What kind of a person do you think I am?!

SAY:
You are wrong to think I would enjoy that... I find what you are saying to be very offensive.

DON'T SAY:
You must really think I'm loose or something!

SAY:
You have no reason to believe I would welcome that.

DON'T SAY:
Where'd you get an idea like that?!

Don't Be Vague Or Misleading

Don't leave yourself open to misinterpretation. Harassers often use the tactic of transforming your words into something sexual that you didn't intend at all. Counter this by saying exactly what you mean. Open-ended remarks that could be turned around to mean something else leave you wide open for more sexually-explicit exchanges.

SAY:
I do not like this conversation and I want it to stop now.

DON'T SAY:
Can't we please talk about something else?

SAY:
Please stop saying that. I am very upset by it.

DON'T SAY:
I don't think this is right, and I don't know what you expect me to say to you.

77

When the Gentle Rebuff
Isn't Enough...

If the person really didn't mean to offend you, one of the Gentle Rebuff responses will probably get him to stop. Be prepared to use it a couple of times. Again, some men find it difficult to believe that a woman means "no," the first time she says it. Even if it's a mistaken belief, many men will choose to discount your refusal as your attempt to be coy about sex. The only way you'll counter this notion is to be firm and consistent in your response.

If your harasser persists beyond a couple of times, you may need to use stronger language to dissuade him. That's what the next chapter, "The Stronger Rebuff" is about. Don't fall into the "I'll-just-give-him-one-last-chance" trap. You owe it to yourself to resolve the situation as promptly as you can, so you can both get on with your jobs.

LEVEL TWO: The Stronger Rebuff

You've told him you object to his behavior, but he continues. Now he's a pest, and he's breaking the law. He needs to be told directly that what he's doing is sexual harassment. Now it's time to use a stronger rebuff. These Level Two responses will show you how to do that. They let your harasser know that you will not tolerate his behavior.

There are times when a Level Two response is appropriate even for a first-time misbehavior. If his language is grossly sexually explicit or disrespectful, or if he has taken liberties with touch, don't hesitate to use strong language to tell him how you feel. You might even find that a Level Three response is warranted, if you consider his behavior to be way out of line. But remember that your personal safety comes first. If you feel threatened, cornered, or in a dangerous situation, don't waste time with verbal responses, get help immediately.

Your ACTION PLAN for The Stronger Rebuff

Guidelines

Firm up the tone of the Gentle Rebuff. Remind him that you've asked him at least *once before* to stop. Tell him that *you* consider his behavior *sexual harassment.* Ask him *again, more firmly* to stop. Don't threaten him.

Action Plan

- Be ready with your rebuff.
- Start documenting the situation. (See Chapter 12.)
- Be prepared to go to the Final Rebuff, if necessary.

Level Two Assertive Responses

SITUATION:
He repeats the offensive comment, innuendo or gesture, or persists in asking you to go out with him.

YOUR RESPONSE:
Be clear in your message and use the exact words "sexual harassment." Few harassers today are ignorant of what a sexual harassment complaint means to their employer, or to their own careers. The words themselves can be a powerful deterrent.

SAY:
I've told you before, I like working with you but I don't want to date you. I consider it sexual harassment when you continue to ask me out when I've already told you NO. Please stop!

SAY:
I told you before... I don't like what you said. This is sexual harassment. Please stop!

SAY:
This is the second (third/fourth) time I've asked you not to touch me that way. This is sexual harassment, and I don't want it to continue.

SITUATION:
He speculates aloud that he thinks you would like to

participate in a certain type of sexual activity (presumably with him.)

YOUR RESPONSE:
Respond directly to his comment by invoking reality, not playing into his fantasies.

> Don't allow remarks like this to go unanswered, because they can quickly escalate. Harassers often use these kinds of speculative comments to "test" your responsiveness and throw you off guard. He wants to pull you into a discussion he can control. Don't let him get away with it.

SAY:
I told you before to stop. This is sexual harassment, and I don't want it to continue.

DON'T SAY:
In your dreams... (or similar sarcastic or slang expressions).

SAY:
I told you before, my personal life has nothing to do with this job. What you are saying is sexual harassment, and I want you to stop.

DON'T SAY:
How could you say something like that to me?!

SITUATION:
He continues to berate you, saying, "Women belong at home, not in this occupation."

81

YOUR RESPONSE:
Don't engage in a debate with him! His theory on women in the workplace is not the issue, and it's no excuse for harassing behavior. Let him know he is offensive and that you are informed about what sexual harassment is and what your rights are.

SAY:
Repeating that offensive remark after I have specifically asked you to stop is sexual harassment. Your behavior is unacceptable. It's affecting my work and I want you to stop it!

SAY:
Once again, what you are doing is sexual harassment. Save us both grief and stop it now!

SITUATION:
He leans close to you and whispers a sexually suggestive remark, as he has done before.

YOUR RESPONSE:
Use your normal speaking voice to tell him immediately to stop.

The conspiratorial nature of harassment situations is reinforced by remarks being made (and responded to) in hushed tones. Don't fall for this. If you really want to embarrass him, repeat his remark out loud so others can hear what he said. If that's too difficult or embarrassing for you, refer to the offensive suggestion as "what you said." The important thing is to let him know you don't intend to participate in his game.

SAY:
What you said is very inappropriate, and I told you before I want you to stop harassing me.

SITUATION:
He asks you to do something sexual to him or for him.

YOUR RESPONSE:
Say "NO" as clearly and directly as you can. Don't talk around the subject, or use euphemisms that he can misinterpret. DO make it clear that his remark is out of line, and that you won't allow it.

SAY:
I told you before not to say that to me, and I meant it. This is sexual harassment, and I will not put up with it.

DON'T SAY:
What a demeaning and horrible thing to say! I'm shocked and offended that someone in your position would dare say something like that to me!

SAY:
I was very specific when I told you before to stop. What you are doing is sexual harassment, and I am telling you again to stop it now.

SAY:
I told you before that I do not want you to continue saying that. I consider this sexual harassment. Please stop right now.

SAY:
This is sexual harassment. I told you before that I will not respond to comments like that. Please stop.

SITUATION:
He repeats a sexual proposition he's made to you before.

YOUR RESPONSE:
Let him know he is jeopardizing his job by engaging in such behavior.

SAY:
You have an important position here. Why are you risking it by continuing to sexually harass me? Please stop it now.

SAY:
You know the company's policy on sexual harassment. Why would you risk being reported by doing something I've told you offends me? Please stop it now.

An Alternative: Put it in Writing

If you feel you really can't confront your harasser in person, you can still say "NO" to him by sending him a memo or letter. Be sure to keep a copy of your letter as evidence.

Writing does help you organize your thoughts better and keep your emotions in check. In some corporate environments, however, such a document could be considered "politically incorrect," even if you're justified in sending it. You can minimize the chance that your letter will hurt your own position by following these simple guidelines:

1. **Be specific in describing the situation.**

   If you're vague, or don't include enough details, your written account might be misinterpreted.

2. **Describe your feelings about what happened.**

   Sometimes people write more formally than they speak, and they tend to leave emotions out of their written accounts. This is a mistake. You want your harasser to know that his words are having a negative impact on you. You'll also want to have this record of your emotions, should you decide to take further action.

3. **State your expectations.**

   Tell him what you expect from him, such as, "I want you to stop leaving sexually explicit messages in my voice mail as of today."

Deliver it in Person

It's a good idea to deliver a written response to your harasser in person so you know for sure that he got the message. You may also want to consider sending him the notice by priority or certified mail. Ask for a delivery confirmation from the post office or delivery service. Be sure to keep the receipt, and the delivery confirmation, with your other documentation.

Example of a Written NO to Your Harasser

MEMORANDUM

DATE:

TO: Your Harasser (include his full name and title)

FROM: Your Name (include your full name and title)

SUBJECT: SEXUAL HARASSMENT

For the past month, you have been leaving messages on my voice mail that are personal and of a sexual nature. I have counted at least five of these messages since the beginning of April. In these messages, you have asked me questions about my sex life and made comments about my body that I find very offensive.

These messages embarrassed and upset me. When I receive one of them, it makes it difficult for me to concentrate on my work. I asked you before to stop. I feel that your behavior is sexual harassment. I want you to stop leaving these messages and I am asking you to keep our relationship on a professional level.

If He Still Doesn't Get It

The stronger rebuffs presented here are designed to stop most harassers. Few men welcome the prospect of being reprimanded for sexual harassment or of losing their jobs because of it. Although sometimes many harassers get away with it, a recent survey of Fortune 500 firms reflects that one in five harassers, who are reported, are fired for sexual harassment.[1] That's a number that would have been unheard of only a few years ago. Employers are realizing that sexual harassment is bad business, and they cannot afford to allow employees to threaten their liability.

There can be exceptions, however. If your harasser is obsessed or hostile, or if he's an Intimidator bent on driving you out of the company, he may not be swayed by the obviously negative consequences. He may feel his power or position makes him immune from being questioned or disciplined. He may not stop harassing you, no matter how strong your company's policy is or how well you handle the situation.

If you're facing this kind of Intimidator, you have one more level of verbal responses to try if you want to resolve the situation on your own. The Final Rebuff responses that follow aren't polite, and they clearly signal your intention to use every response available to you to stop your harasser.

If your situation has reached this level, now's the time to seriously consider acquiring some allies who

---

1.   Bravo, Ellen and Ellen Cassady. *The 9to5 Guide to Combating Sexual Harassment.* New York: Wiley & Sons, 1992.

can help you. "The Power of Involving Others," beginning on page 130, can tell you how.

You may have to draw on your courage to confront your harasser in person, or in writing, but you will feel much better about yourself for doing so. It's very rewarding to know you've dealt with a difficult situation in a mature and competent manner. The skills you gain as you become more assertive can aid you in managing other aspects of your life, too.

LEVEL THREE: The Final Rebuff

LEVEL THREE: The Final Rebuff

The responses offered here give your harasser one last opportunity to stop—before you report his illegal behavior to others in the company or decide to take even stronger action. Relatively few harassers persist to this level, but those who do are responsible for most of the sexual harassment lawsuits and complaints filed with the EEOC or other state agencies.

Should you find yourself facing an individual who won't stop harassing you, you'd be wise to confide in someone else about your situation. Having someone else within your company aware of your situation helps you feel you're not alone in trying to resolve the harassment, and it also gives you a strategic advantage should your harasser force you to take further action against him.

Should you warn him that you are giving him one last chance before you take action? Should you actually confront your harasser with a specific action, like threatening to report him to his boss, or filing a lawsuit against him and the company? These are tough choices that depend on your judgment of the situation. Before you decide, here are some things you ought to consider.

Up Against the Wall

A harasser may pay attention to your warning. Your final threat of action might be the ultimate defense that brings him to his senses. It could also have the opposite effect.

Revealing your plan of action could cause your harasser to strike first in an attempt to destroy your

89

credibility. He could, for example, make up stories that cast doubt on your behavior. He might imply that you're angry because he jilted you, or he might be critical of your work performance and try to link it to your accusations against him. He might also try to use the charge against you that Anita Hill heard: that maybe you're fantasizing the whole thing.

Don't assume your harasser won't try to retaliate against you. His ego isn't all that's at stake, and both of you know it. You'll want to think through the benefits and consequences of your situation before you make the decision to tell him you plan to report him officially. The chapters in Section III can help you assess your own risks.

On the other hand, if you threaten him with further action but don't follow through, you will be powerless against his next attack, and you will run a very high risk that he'll be back to torment you again. Remember that this is a person who has previously disregarded your specific requests to stop the harassment. He's not likely to cooperate with you if you show the slightest indication that you will back down from your promise of action.

If you do decide to report him, please make a copy of your employee records beforehand, so that you can guard against the possibility that he or someone else will tamper with them. Keep these copies in a safe place.

Common Retorts from Harassers

If you're facing situations like those described here, you're probably beyond the point of expecting your harasser to be reasonable. Even if he eventually stops harassing you, he may respond defensively and say something negative to you to try to shake your resolve or catch you off-guard.

It's important to remember that retaliatory remarks don't require a response. Engaging in debate or exchanging insults or accusations with your harasser won't resolve anything, and it can weaken your own defense. Just stick to the consistent, direct approach you've been using with him all along. Don't argue over motivations, ulterior motives, or threats. And if he says something personally hurtful, try to keep it in perspective because he's on the defensive.

Here are some typical comments your harasser may try to use:

SOME TYPICAL COMMENTS BY HARASSERS

- You don't know what you're talking about.
- I don't know what you are talking about.
- You must be imagining things.
- You misread my intentions.
- You must have a whopping case of PMS.
- I think you're bluffing.
- I could care less what you think, you're nothing.
- I am the boss around here, and I call the shots, not you.
- You're overreacting.

- You're a hysterical female.
- You're a bitch.
- You're upset because I jilted you.
- You're upset because you didn't get that raise.
- Your career will be over.
- You just hate men.
- You just need a good screw.
- You made me do it.
- You women are all the same, just out to get men.
- No one will believe you.

Your ACTION PLAN for The Final Rebuff

Guidelines

Firm up the tone of the Stronger Rebuff. Remind him that you asked him at least ***twice before*** to stop. Tell him that his behavior is ***sexual harassment*** and it's unlawful, and that he's putting ***his job at risk. Demand*** that he stop. ***Consider carefully*** if you want to reveal your follow-up action plan.

Action Plan

- Be ready with your final rebuff.
- Involve others, if you can.
- Be up-to-date with your documentation.
- Be prepared to act and follow through immediately. (See Section III)

Level Three Assertive Responses

SITUATION:

He continues or escalates the behavior that you have repeatedly told him you find offensive.

YOUR RESPONSE:

Let him know that his behavior is sexual harassment and it's unlawful. Speak firmly and clearly. Demand that he stop immediately.

SAY:

I asked you twice before to stop this offensive behavior.

This is sexual harassment and it's unlawful. I demand that you stop saying these things now!

SAY:
I have made it clear before that your behavior is offensive to me. This is unlawful behavior. It is sexual harassment and I want you to stop it immediately!

SITUATION:
He threatens you with retaliation.

YOUR RESPONSE:
Threatening to retaliate against you is an attempt to intimidate you by making you responsible for the situation. Don't allow his threats to sidetrack you from your response. Make him directly responsible by letting him know that his behavior is the problem, not yours.

SAY:
I am only concerned about what you are doing to me right now. I have told you repeatedly to stop, but you won't. This is sexual harassment and I will not tolerate it any longer.

SAY:
I am not the person breaking the law, you are. I warned you twice before that I consider your behavior to be sexual harassment. It's unlawful and unwelcome. I demand that you stop it now!

NOTE: If you've already made the decision to take further action against your harasser if he doesn't stop, and if you feel prepared to do so, you might add a specific promise of action to the above response.

SAY:
What you are doing to me is illegal. If you touch me again, you will leave me no alternative but to report you to corporate headquarters for sexual harassment.

SITUATION:
He keeps denying that it's sexual harassment (or implies you have other motives for accusing him of harassment).

YOUR RESPONSE:
Such denial by harassers is common. Don't allow his insinuations to sway you. State the facts, repeat your feelings and refuse to enter into a debate with him. (It's your option if you want to warn him of further action you'll take if he doesn't stop immediately.)

SAY:
Regardless of how you feel about it, I've told you several times before that I consider your behavior to be sexual harassment, and I will not tolerate it. Your behavior is unlawful and I demand that it stop now!

SAY:
I've already told you that this is unprofessional behavior. I will not allow you to continue sexually harassing me. If you don't stop immediately, I am prepared to report what you are doing to (name his boss).

SITUATION:
He attacks your credibility or says that no one would believe you.

YOUR RESPONSE:
This is often a highly emotional exchange, because your integrity is being questioned. Try to stay calm, if you can. Deflect his verbal attacks or threats with a firm restatement of the real facts. Refuse to be drawn into a discussion about your credibility or who's to blame for the situation.

SAY:
My credibility is not the issue, and you know it. Your behavior is the issue. What you are doing to me is sexual harassment, and it is illegal. I told you I will not allow you to continue treating me in this way, and I mean it.

SITUATION:
He threatens to tell others you are trying to seduce him.

YOUR RESPONSE:
Don't be distracted. Link your plan to take action with the law or company policy.

SAY:
The real issue here is your behavior towards me. There are laws to protect me against sexual harassment, and I know what they are. I have told you repeatedly to stop. You are violating company policy, and you are risking your job by refusing to stop harassing me.

95

SAY:

You may tell others whatever you wish, but I've told you before to stop harassing me. Your behavior is sexual harassment; it's unlawful, and I demand that you stop it!

SAY:

I will not have my job or my reputation at this company threatened by you any longer. If you ever speak to me in that way again, I will file a formal complaint against you for sexual harassment.

SITUATION:

He tells you that you can't "prove" anything. There are no witnesses, you have no evidence, etc.

YOUR RESPONSE:

Again, his behavior is the real issue, not whether you can prove he did it. Let him know that, in fact, you do have documentation of every incident of harassment, and that you will not hesitate to involve others if he doesn't stop the behavior.

SAY:

Proof isn't the issue. Your behavior toward me is what we are discussing. I told you several times since you began this sexual harassment that your behavior is unacceptable to me. I demand that you stop it immediately!

SAY:

As a matter of fact, I have plenty of evidence. I have copies of the obscene messages you left on my phone, and a journal I've kept about the things you've said to me at work. If you ever sexually harass me again, I will use this evidence against you.

SAY:

I won't allow you to intimidate me like this. If you ever touch me again, or if you threaten me in any way, I will go to company officials with the documentation I have on you.

What's Next?

If you've responded assertively to your harasser using the principles outlined in this chapter and he continues to harass you, he's made a conscious decision to break the law. Now you'll have to consider taking further action to get him to stop or to remove yourself from the situation.

You don't necessarily have to file a formal complaint against your harasser, but if you decide to do so, you will need some help. You'll need to find out who in your company has the responsibility to help you and how you can best present your case. The next section will tell you what you need to know to build evidence and enlist someone with power on your side.

Whether or not you actually go through the steps of a formal investigation, it is valuable to know specifically how to file a complaint with your employer, request a formal investigation by a state agency, or pursue a lawsuit. In Section III, "When Words Fail," you'll find candid discussions on the pros and cons of taking your complaint to this level, plus practical advice to help you in your decision.

Chapter 9

DANGER SIGNALS

Protecting Yourself from Physical Harm

S exual harassment rarely results in physical assault or rape, but you should be alert to that possibility. If you have a gut feeling that you're in physical danger from your harasser, saying "no" may not be enough—get away and get help immediately.

Sometimes, women feel they can put up with anything rather than risk losing their job. I remember the story of a 62-year-old inventory clerk who had been sexually molested by a supervisor in his twenties. Apparently, this supervisor knew that she needed her job so badly that she wasn't likely to say anything against him. For months, she endured from this young man some of the most egregious forms of sexual harassment and physcial abuse on the job I've ever heard described.

Fortunately, a co-worker discovered what was happening and offered to back up her story with the company owner. The supervisor was disciplined and then transferred to another store, but the inventory clerk still remembers vividly the humiliation and self-loathing she experienced. It affected her for the rest of her working life.

Your own situation may not be so severe, but it's worth being cautious. Sexual harassment is never a neutral situation, especially for the victim. Pay particular attention to signals from your harasser that his come-ons are getting stronger, or that he's willing to take more risks to confront you.

This is what happened to Clarissa. Hers is a very poignant story. I'm including it here so you'll be aware that there's always the possibility that harassment can get dangerously out of control.

Clarrissa's Story
Age 29, Computer Programmer

For months, he'd been making comments to me and telling me how sexy he thought I was. I told him it made me uncomfortable and that I wasn't attracted to him in that way. I tried to ignore it but he just kept it up. He never missed an opportunity to touch me in some way—but always real sneaky-like. He'd help me on with my coat and then make sure he brushed off some imaginary lint so he could touch me on my breasts or on the butt. If I said something, he acted innocent, like he didn't know what I was talking about. Right after Christmas, I started keeping a little log whenever he'd pull stuff like that. At the time, I just wanted to figure out how often he was doing it—I wasn't really thinking about turning him in. Actually, I really thought I could handle it myself.

The incident that changed everything was something I probably should have seen coming. He had cornered me in the break room earlier that week and I'd gotten pretty mad at him. I told him I thought what he was doing was sex harassment and I was tired of putting up with it. He told me I was having fantasies about sex.

A couple of days later, I got on the freight elevator and there he was. As soon as the door closed, he backed me up against the wall and started trying to kiss me and put his hands all over me. I was shocked out of my mind. It was clear he wasn't playing around, and I didn't know what he might do. I really thought he was going to rape me right there in the company freight elevator.

I couldn't believe it was happening. All I could think about was that here was somebody I'd worked with for over five years—somebody I had once respected and liked and once thought of as a great boss—coming on to me like some creep. I shoved him away from me and told him to never, ever come near me again—I was just screaming at him as loud as I could. I was hysterical.

When the door opened, a bunch of guys from the receiving dock were standing there, trying to find out what was going on. I just tore out of there and went straight to the Personnel Office and told them what happened.

He denied he was trying to rape me, of course. The guys from receiving hadn't really seen anything, so there weren't any witnesses. The company didn't fire him, but he was put on disciplinary probation, and of course everybody knew about it. It was the number one topic of conversation around there. I took a transfer to another department, so he's not my boss anymore. I see him sometimes, but he never speaks to me unless he has to. Basically, we just avoid being anywhere near each other.

I can't believe it happened to me, and I still wonder if I did something that just made him snap or something. But I'm glad I reported him, and I'd do it again in a second. You just can't let guys like that get away with it or nobody would be safe around here. Somebody has to let them know they can't do anything they want.

Protect Yourself

If you have any reason to suspect that your harasser intends you physical harm, report your suspicions immediately to the head of personnel, or to the appropriate supervisor within your company. Demand that they help you come up with a solution that will keep you safe. Don't hesitate to seek help.

If you're caught by surprise by someone who tries to physically take advantage of you, make as much noise as you can, to attract the attention of others. If you can't get away from him yourself, scream, break something, push over the bookcase or do whatever it takes to bring attention to the situation. Here are some common-sense strategies you should follow:

- Be alert to situations in which your harasser is maneuvering to get you alone. Don't play games of hide-and-seek, but be sensible about situations in which you'll be alone with him.

- When the meeting adjourns, collect your materials and leave quickly.

- If he singles you out at the meeting and asks you to wait while the others leave, ask someone to wait with you. Or leave anyway.

- If everyone in the office is car-pooling to the company function, make sure you go in someone else's car. If he asks (or orders) you to ride with him, decline. No one is going to fire you for refusing a ride in his car.

- If he asks you to come in early or stay late, suggest an alternate time when you know others will be around.

These are interim strategies only, and on their own, they probably won't protect you from harassment. Using avoidance as a long-term solution doesn't work, either. You'll be on edge, your work will suffer, and you'll weaken your position with your employer, especially since the level of stress over the harassment often causes problems in performance.

Treat the possibility of physical danger in the workplace seriously. Sexual harassment most often happens behind closed doors or away from others. Underestimating your harasser's intent is a serious mistake you should avoid. As I've said throughout this book, please trust your own instincts. No job is worth the risk of your personal safety.

What's Ahead

In Section II, we discussed assertive skills and verbal techniques for stopping sexual harassment.

In Section III, we're going to examine what happens when your harasser won't stop. You have rights and choices, not the least of which are strong laws to protect victims of sexual harassment. But there are risks involved as well. It's not an easy decision for any of us.

Before making that decision, it's smart to consider what's ahead.

SECTION III

WHEN WORDS FAIL

Introduction

If you've tried every assertive response to reason with your harasser, and he's still harassing you, you could be facing some difficult choices. No doubt you're feeling anger, frustration, and a whole gamut of emotional responses to what he's doing to you and your job security. You may feel you want to do anything and everything you can to get him to stop.

In the midst of such conflict and strong emotions, it's understandable to want revenge or to just want to escape. But what you need now is to be realistic about your situation. Now's the time to set your emotions aside and carefully examine your options. Unfortunately, the rights and choices available to you don't come without certain risks. This chapter, and the ones that follow, will explore the pros and cons of each of your options, so you can make a more informed decision.

If your harasser won't stop, you have several options:

- You can choose silence.

- You can quit your job.

- You can take further action by documenting each incident and finding witness and/or allies.

- You can ask a supervisor or manager to intervene, and seek the support of co-workers.

- You can file a formal complaint with your employer, using the procedures established by your company.

- You can file a complaint with the Equal Employment Opportunity Commission (EEOC) or a state agency, if your company can't or won't resolve the situation.

- You can file a lawsuit against your harasser and the employer.

Some of these options are obvious. You could say nothing, and hope your harasser either gives up, gets transferred, or miraculously vanishes off the face of the earth. Quitting your job would immediately stop the direct harassment, of course, but what are the consequences to you?

The rights of victims of sexual harassment are protected under federal and state antidiscrimination laws. Since these laws place the responsibility for sexual harassment on the employer, your company probably has some kind of antidiscrimination policy in place to offer its employees (and itself) protection as well. Yet even the strongest of laws or the most stringent of policies can't help you if you don't choose to use them. Choosing to exercise your rights means understanding the system and knowing how to take action—whether you're taking your complaint to someone in your company, to an outside agency, or to a private attorney.

Chapter 10

THE RISKS OF CHOOSING SILENCE

The High Cost of Choosing Silence

Many of us choose silence. In a 1992 *Working Woman* report, 46% of the more than 9,000 women surveyed said that their most common response to the problem of sexual harassment is to try to ignore it.

Why do so many women favor this approach? Marya's story says a lot about the high cost of choosing silence:

Marya's Story
Age 38, Physicist

Some of the women I know think of sexual harassment as something they don't worry about or as a problem only in business circles. I hear a lot of big talk from them. They think that if somebody gives you trouble, you should turn the guy in or just quit.

It's just not always that easy. I know what Anita Hill went through. When I was in graduate school, my advisor was one of the celebrity faculty members, a distinguished scholar who had written tons of books and articles and was considered by many to be in the running for a Nobel. Professionally, he was up there with the saints. I knew something else about him.

He used to talk to me about sex all the time. He would tell me he had these erotic fantasies with me in them, and he'd tell me in detail what they were. These were very graphic fantasies. It made my skin crawl. Sometimes he'd also force me to perform oral sex on him in the laboratory late at night. He'd lock the door and push me down on the floor beneath the tables and make me do it to him. There was never any question about turning him in. He made it quite clear to me that if I ever told anybody about it, he would ruin my career.

I haven't seen him in years, but he's still the most prominent name in my field of science, and I still fear reprisals from him. I'm still in psychologocial counseling over this experience.

At first thought, silence might seem to pose the least risk to your career. When you choose silence, you choose not to risk possible retaliation from your harasser, if you report him. You may spare yourself the possibility that your company might force you out, if your complaint stirs up the corporate waters, or if it prompts them to decide between you. You save yourself the grief of counter-accusations, gossip, and co-workers who may ostracize you.

Yet unfortunately, your silence serves your harasser, too. It tells him, in effect, that he can continue to act abusively without fear of consequences. There is nothing to stop him from continuing, and even escalating, his behavior if he chooses.

Your silence also allows discriminatory practices to remain unchallenged. Many corporations defend their inadequate prevention or reporting policies by saying that few women come forward with complaints. The people in charge assume that: "If we don't hear anything, it must not be that big of a problem," or "Our policy works." But the reality is that the reporting system and the suspicion that greet such complaints often make it extremely difficult for victims to come forward.

Is There a Downside for You?

Yes. Allowing your harasser to continue unchallenged can leave you feeling not only humiliated and powerless, but also less sure of yourself. You may find that your concentration and judgment are impaired, or that you're not doing the same quality of work as before. You may also take yourself out of the running for advancement, because you begin to question your own ability to do the job.

"A woman in these difficult and stressful situations needs to choose wisely," advises psychologist Debra Borys. "In reviewing your decision about what to do, you need to acknowledge the impact your decision will have on your sense of competence. Anything you can do to regain control over the situation is a positive step to preserving self-esteem."[1]

---

1.   Borys, Debra. Interview with author. Los Angeles, CA, 1992.

Physical and Mental Health Concerns

Aside from the emotional turmoil that you may experience at work, you may find yourself suffering health problems as a result of not confronting the problem. Feeling out of control, or helpless, brings on depression for many women. Physical symptoms may surface, too.

Dr. Mary Kay O'Neill, a physician at Seattle's Virginia Mason Clinic, notes that physical ailments such as chronic headaches, backaches, sleep disruption, fatigue, eating disorders, and even chronic pelvic pain, can be linked to stress. She sees a connection between stress and the body's ability to resist some diseases, especially those that attack the immune system.

Dr. O'Neill advises women who are facing stressful situations at work to be attentive to changes in their health, and to be candid in discussing these situations with their doctor.[2]

Personal and Professional Relationships

The inner conflicts you face when you try to endure sexual harassment in silence is bound to color your other professional relationships. You may find yourself becoming hypersensitive to comments that others may make, or you may feel so compromised that you pull away from normal social interactions you used to enjoy.

---

2.   O'Neill, Mary Kay, M.D. Interview with author. Seattle, WA, 1992.

111

If your colleagues know that you're being singled out for sexual attention, particularly by a superior, your silence may cause them to think you welcome the behavior. This could result in questions about your integrity or your character.

You're also likely to bring the stress home with you and find that it affects your personal relationships, too.

Suzannah's Story
Age 30, Media Relations Specialist

I couldn't even repeat some of the things this guy said to me at work. I tried to tell my husband about it, and he thought I was making it up. The first thing he said was, "What did you have on?" He thinks no man would say things like to that to a women unless she did something to make him think it was okay. I guess my husband thinks I'm leading this guy on or that it's all my fault.

Stories like Suzannah's aren't unusual. They feed into the self-blame syndrome that can prevent victims from speaking out. Don't allow your partner to make you feel worse about yourself. If he or she can't be supportive, choose a friend, family member or counselor who can be. In your anger at your harasser, you may need to find some outlet to avoid venting your rage on the people who matter most to you.

Making the Best of Silence

You do pay a price when you choose silence. Yet for some of us, there is no other option. You may decide that your job is so crucial to your career or to your economic survival, that you simply can't risk losing it, regardless of how you feel about the harassment. If this is your decision, here are some positive ways you can live with it:

Keep it Confidential

If you've decided not to confront your harasser or inform your employer about the situation, don't discuss it with co-workers on or off the job. People do talk, and sexual harassment is just too irresistible a subject for gossip.

You run two risks in discussing the case "unofficially." First, your conversation could get back to someone in management. They might consider your allegations false, since you haven't "gone through channels" to report it. Even the suspicion by top management that you are falsely accusing someone of sexual harassment can have a very serious impact on your career.

Second, talking about your harassment without doing anything about it can make you look like a whiner or a complainer who won't defend herself. You won't get much support or understanding if you give people this impression of you.

Consider a Transfer or Reassignment

If you work for a larger company, there may be suitable openings in another department or branch. Find out what's available, and consider whether you'd have long-term benefits from the move. This could give you an opportunity to "start fresh," and may help you put the harassment behind you.

Try to Refocus Your Attention

Even if you remain in your current job, you may be eligible for retraining or assignment to a new project that interests you. You may feel more positive about your job, and yourself, if you can put your energies into something that will allow you to shift your focus away from the sexual harassment.

Seek Outside Help

Call a self-help hotline, join a support group or engage a qualified therapist. You may need some outlet for the rage, frustration and fear you are not able to express at work.

Be Kind to Yourself

Your decision to remain silent is your choice. Once you've chosen it, put the agony of making that decision behind you and get on with your life. If you continue to suffer anxieties or self-doubts that affect your job performance or disrupt your personal life, perhaps you may want to consider some of the options discussed in the next few chapters.

And remember, you can always change your mind.

Chapter 11

SHOULD YOU QUIT?

Despite the strong laws against sexual harassment, justice doesn't always prevail in the workplace. Sometimes, the victim suffers while the harasser loses nothing.

Studies show that as many as one in four women who experience sexual harassment quit their jobs over it.[1] (If the statisticians are right, that means that seven million American women could quit their jobs this year because of sexual harassment!)

The U.S. Department of Labor statistics are based on the number of women who quit their jobs over a lifetime. Some women may quit two or three times because of sexual harassment. Others may quit and give another reason, even though they might have been considered part of the original percentage of victims.

Walking out, even before you have another job, can bring immediate emotional satisfaction. Down the road, however, it can also create financial hardship. Here's why:

---

1. Estimated statistics based on U.S. Department of Labor, Bureau of Labor Statistics. 1989.

115

Time Spent Out of Work

How long it takes you to find a new job depends on a number of variables. Women seeking mid-level positions can expect to spend between two and nine months or longer interviewing for a new job, depending on the industry. If the economy is in a recession, the search can take even longer.

If your field of expertise is science or high technology, being out of the job market even a few months can result in you falling behind your colleagues. The competition for top level jobs is especially tough in these fields.

If you're seeking a professional or executive position, your wait can be even longer. In general, the higher the job level, the smaller the job market, and the tighter the competition. Julie Prafke, a human resources specialist, who owns an *Inc. Magazine* "Top 500" temporary employment service says, "If you live in a small or rural community or have skills in a specialized area, your opportunities may be further limited. For women of color, the search can be considerably longer."[2]

If you can't afford to be out of work for long, you may be forced to accept a job that is less skilled or is lower in pay and benefits than your present job. You may also have to pay out of your own pocket the cost of retraining for a new position.

---

2.   Julie Prafke, President of Humanix, Inc. Interview with author, Spokane, WA, 1992.

If you find it necessary to relocate to find a comparable job, a move will definitely cause upheaval in your personal life. You'll probably have to pay the interview or travel expenses yourself, and you may incur some, if not all, of the cost of your move.

Long-Term Financial Impact

If you work for a large corporation, you may have an investment in a pension or retirement plan. If you quit, you may forfeit much of the money set aside for your retirement. Be sure to find out what your options are if you withdraw from the plan your current employer has provided.

"In some cases, you could lose 100% of what you've contributed, if certain conditions aren't met," says Charles Keturakat, a financial and investment specialist with Principal Financial Group. "Most investment and benefit programs have strict guidelines and restrictions covering ex-employees. You need to read them carefully. Even if you're able to retain your healthcare or benefits package, you'll be responsible for the monthly premiums. Depending on the coverage, and how may family members you include, that could cost you several hundred dollars per month."[3]

"If you do have retirement money coming to you after you leave your job, be sure to invest it in time," says tax attorney Tom Culbertson. "If you're under age 59-1/2, you must roll over or reinvest all monies from a 401k plan within 60 days. If you don't roll over into

---

3. Keturakat, Charles. Interview with author, Spokane, WA, 1992.

another 401k plan or a personal IRA within that time, you could be hit with substantial penalties ad additional taxes."[4]

Here's an example of what this could mean to you in real dollars: If you have $10,000 invested in a 401k with your employer and need to withdraw that money to support yourself while you're looking for a new job, you could end up with only $5,900 of the original amount you had invested.[5] Withdrawing these funds means you'll lose the benefit of all the compound interest you would have accumulated. Worse, you'll have less money to live on after you retire.

Making the Best of Saying Goodbye

You may decide that leaving your job is still your best option, despite the financial impact it could have on you. Maintaining your self-respect is certainly a valid consideration. You may also feel that the daily battle with your harasser is too wearing on you emotionally. And quitting does not mean that you have to give up your attempts to seek redress against your company, either by filing a complaint with the appropriate government agency or filing a private lawsuit.

---

4. Culbertson, Tom. Interview with author, Spokane, WA, 1992.
5. Based on a 31% tax bracket. These things get complicated, so check with your financial advisor or your company's corporate officer to confirm the exact status of your personal situation.

If you do decide to quit without lining up another job first, the following suggestions can help you.

Starting Over: Interview With Finesse

What do you say to prospective employers who ask why you left your job? Personnel and executive search specialists say that admitting you left a job because of sexual harassment can be absolutely lethal to your chances of being hired.

Even though 80% of us leave our jobs for personal reasons, you don't necessarily need to say that sexual harassment was your reason for leaving. If a sharp interviewer probes why you left, here are some good answers to that question.

SAY:
I had hoped my last position would offer me an environment that would encourage the best of my work experience and skills. Unfortunately, that didn't turn out to be the case.

SAY:
I enjoyed my work at my last job, but other factors weren't compatible. I want to work in a professional environment that's based on respect for each individual and what they can contribute. My last job didn't provide that.

Taking the Direct Approach

If you feel you can talk candidly with your interviewer about the sexual harassment situation you left, try to frame your decision to leave in the best light possible.

119

It's not necessary to be accusatory or hostile toward your old employer. These responses show your professionalism and personal integrity.

SAY:

It was difficult for me to leave my job, but I was unwilling to continue working in an environment that I felt did not respect my professionalism about my work. If I could have transferred to another location or department, it might have been different, but under the circumstance, I felt it wiser to resign.

SAY:

Although my previous employer had a policy against sexual harassment, I felt that filing a formal complaint against the person who was harassing me would have been counter-productive to my career. I have excellent skills and I want the opportunity to utilize them in a positive and professional work environment.

Exploring New Career Paths

Changing your focus from a career that's been interrupted to one that's headed in a new direction can be a positive step toward recovery. If your situation permits, you might want to use this interim period for healing and personal exploration. Consider trying something new, or more challenging. Assessing your priorities and regenerating your spirit can make you stronger as you go forward.

If you don't feel up to the rigors of a formal job search, or if you want to explore a variety of new fields that interest you, consider signing on with a reputable temporary agency. Temporary job assignments give you flexibility and variety. The better firms also offer benefits packages, paid vacations, and even pension plans.

You can usually command a higher rate of pay, and often a more skilled assignment when you work as a temporary employee, rather than accept a part-time job. A temporary job will also give you the opportunity to check out a particular company to see whether you'd like to become a permanent employee there.

Don't assume that all temporary assignments are clerical. Some agencies place their temporaries in highly skilled administrative or supervisory positions. Others specialize in placing people in sales, manufacturing or light industrial jobs.

Returning to School

Don't overlook the value of going back to school for retraining. Explore new markets for your existing skills. Many communities offer high-quality adult education programs. Finishing a degree program, gaining new skills, or satisfying your intellectual curiosity can be wonderfully rewarding and healing.

Returning to school may also be more affordable than you think. Ask the financial aid officer at the institution you're considering about loans and scholarships that may be available to you. In addition to numerous financial aid programs available to all students with need, some schools offer special aid programs specifically designated for women returning to school.

Allow Yourself All the Support You Need

Seeking out others who share your interests and concerns can help you through this transitional period. Individual counseling may help you grow beyond the experience much more quickly than you would alone. The right support group can also help you recover. You'll find that you are not alone, and that you have much to contribute, which is a wonderful thing to discover about yourself when you're feeling low.

Chapter 12

ENHANCING YOUR CREDIBILITY

The Importance of Documentation

O ne of the biggest obstacles to standing up to sexual harassment is the fear that no one will believe you.

If you suspect that you'll need to build a case against your harasser, there are two very effective ways to enhance your credibility. One is by **documenting** the incidents in writing or on tape. Another is by seeking **witnesses**, or **allies**, to support you. Both of these are important elements in your defense strategy.

Documentation: The Power of Putting it in Writing

At the beginning of this book, I suggested that you keep a personal journal to help you begin thinking assertively about sexual harassment. Writing down your reactions, ideas, and opinions is a very useful way to validate your feelings, gain perspective, and confirm your decisions. For many of us, it's comforting to write things down.

However, when you find yourself facing a situation that requires a stronger rebuff, you need to begin another kind of journal—a carefully prepared record that documents the sexual harassment you are experiencing. It may take some discipline on your part, but I cannot overemphasize how important documentation can be to you. *It not only helps your credibility with others, it could very well be the deciding factor in how your situation is resolved.*

Documentation provides primary evidence of people, places, events, and your reactions to them at the time they are happening. A clearly-written, highly-detailed, accurate chronology of your situation is the strongest tool you will ever have in case you need to take action against your harasser.

Legal professionals call it contemporaneous evidence, and it's a key factor in virtually every lawsuit involving sexual harassment. Literally, the term means, "as it happens." The more contemporaneous the documentation, the more valuable it is to your case. Consider your documentation journal as if it were your insurance policy.

Most attorneys believe that your contemporaneous evidence is vital if you pursue a lawsuit. You can easily undermine yourself in a court if you rely on memory alone.

Here are some important things about documentation you need to know.

Write it Down Right Away–You Really Do Forget

Immediate recall is adversely affected by a stressful situation. Because sexual harassment is so stressful, it's difficult to remember later the specific details of an incident as it evolved. Yet it's the details which can make or break your case as a plaintiff, says Aaron R.

Petersen, a lawyer who has worked as a public prosecutor and as a defense attorney on numerous discrimination cases.

"Saying it happened sometime last month, or maybe last Wednesday just isn't good enough," says Petersen. "The other side will be looking to challenge everything you say about the situation, including your recollection of events. Having a journal with dated entries and details about events as they happened is of strategic importance to your case."[1]

You'll do yourself the greatest good by documenting what happened to you as soon as you can, while your memory of details is still fresh. Write down everything you can remember: the date, the time it happened, where it happened, who was involved, who might have witnessed the behavior, and exactly what was said or done. Add specific details, such as what people were wearing, how loudly they spoke, where both of you were standing or sitting in relation to one another, and what you said in response. Include as many details as you can, to build believability into your account. Also include the names and reactions of persons you may have told about the harassment.

Stick to the Facts

Don't try to speculate on your harasser's motivations or why you think this happened. *The fact* that it happened is more important than *why* it happened, especially if it's been repeated. Try to relate the conversation exactly

---

1.   Petersen, Aaron. R. Interview with author. Spokane, WA, 1992.

as you remember it, and don't summarize events or mince words. If he used profanity or explicit sexual terms, write down exactly what he said so that there can be no misinterpretation later. Again, the more details you include, the better record it will provide.

Include Your Emotions

This is very important. We often try to eliminate our emotions when we write formally, but in this case, you should include them. Describe how you felt before, during, and after the encounter, and how you feel the incident affected your emotions, your mental or physical health, or the way you performed your job.

Documentation Checklist

Each of your journal entries should contain the following information:

- The date the entry was written or recorded.
- The date and the time the harassment incident occurred.
- Where the incident occurred (be specific).
- The complete name, title, position, and department of your harasser.
- Witnesses. (Include names, titles, positions, and any other pertinent details.)
- What happened in full detail, including:
  exact words used;
  description of gestures or physical posture;
  descriptions of tone of voice, dress, mannerisms;
  attitude.
- How you responded at the time.
- How your harasser responded at the time.
- How you felt about the harassment.
- Person(s) you told about it and when you told them.

Help With Documentation

Sometimes you can be so angry or frustrated, when you begin to document an incident, that you don't even know where to start. Use this handy form as a guide to set up your documentation journal. It will help you remember to include the pertinent details that provide the best evidence of what happened.

DOCUMENTATION JOURNAL ENTRY

Today's Date _____

Date Incident Occurred _____

Time Incident Occurred _____

Place Incident Occurred_____

Name of Harasser _____

Title_____

Department/Division/Area _____

Witnesses or Others Aware of Incident (Names, Titles, Positions)

_____

_____

What Happened _____

_____

_____

Your Response _____

_____

Harasser's Response_____

_____

How You Felt About It _____

_____

Additional Comments _____

Save Everything Related to the Harassment

If your harasser leaves you a note, sends you a letter or memo, sticks a cartoon or poster on your desk or locker, or gives you anything that you think is related to his harassment campaign, be sure to save it. Attach a label noting the date, time, and details of how or when you received it. Keep a record of these in your documentation journal.

The same thing applies, in this electronic age, to computerized mailbox or voice mail messages, answering machine messages, or those sexually suggestive comments he may have inserted into his dictation tape. Make copies of these if you can. If that's not possible, transcribe the messages, note the date, time and details, and include them with your documentation. All of these things are evidence, and they are very incriminating against your harasser.

Keep the Documentation Separate and Safe

Attorney Petersen also recommends that you keep your documentation on the harassment separate from any other personal journal or diary you may keep.[2] There's a good reason for this: entries concerning your private life—including comments about dates or personal relationships—are only important if they relate directly to the harassment situation. They could potentially be used against you.

Finally, you should be extremely cautious about where you record the information. Your documentation

---

2. Petersen, Aaron R. Interview with author. Spokane, WA, 1992.

journal is a very private and very incriminating document. It could create severe repercussions for you and others. Be very careful about creating computer documents or written reports at work, where others may have access to them. Make a backup copy of any computer journal, and take it off-site. Make a copy of a written journal at an outside copy shop. (Don't risk using the office copy machine.) Keep your documentation journal and the copies at home or in a safe place to insure that your journal stays private.

NOTE: *If writing things down in long hand is a problem for you, or if you'd prefer not to use your computer or word processor to document events, try speaking into a tape recorder. The medium isn't important; what's important is that you take the time to record what happened.*

Chapter 13

SEEKING HELP INSIDE YOUR COMPANY

The Power of Involving Others

Reaching out to others can help you in two ways. The right people can give you support and encouragement, and they can also corroborate your version of events and reliably report on your emotional state if you need this kind of support later on. Just talking with someone who is able to listen to you and sympathize with your situation can help calm you, and make you feel stronger.

Friends, relatives or outsiders can also help bring a fresh perspective to the situation you face every day at work. If you find a co-worker you feel you can trust, do so; but try to minimize your conversations about the situation while you're on the job. It's better if you can meet away from the office.

A sympathetic colleague can really be a valuable support for you. A co-worker is usually familiar with your workplace environment and knows the people involved. He or she may also be able to help steer you through the confusion of corporate politics when you're trying to decide whether or not to involve the company.

Harassers often follow patterns of behavior, and they're not always discreet. Even if no one has approached you about it, it's quite likely that some of your co-workers may have seen your harasser in action or may have overheard you when you asked him to stop. Witnesses not only help strengthen your case, they can be a source of strength and validation for you.

Bear in mind, however, that sometimes a request like this can put your co-worker or office-mate in a very difficult position. Some people refuse to get involved in sexual harassment situations, even when they know the truth about an incident or have experienced it themselves. They may feel it is politically risky, or not in their own career interest to support you. You may have felt this way yourself at one time or another.

You may also discover that your harasser is bothering other women at work. They may be more willing than you think to support you. Here's a wonderful example of the power of group cooperation:

Monica's Story
Age 30, Bank Teller

He was a vice president and he'd been with the bank for over 15 years. Everybody knew this guy had a reputation for hitting on the tellers. He was like a little bee—going from one flower to another—just a real pest. It was unbelievable the stuff women put up with from him, I guess because they were afraid to say anything to him. Then one day, the girls got together and started talking about what we could do about him. Every single person in that group had an experience with him.

We decided we would put him in his place once and for all. So we planned this deal where the next time he tried to hit on any one of us, whoever it was would let everybody know and call his bluff. And that's what happened. He made some comment to me about wanting me to bend over his desk so he could see if my books were in balance, and I said in a real loud voice: "Hey you guys, guess what Charlie just said to me?" And then I just repeated it exactly like he'd said it so everyone around me could hear.

There was silence in the whole bank, like everything came to a complete stop and everyone just stared at him. You should have seen the look on his face. He never bothered any of us again. The thing that really amazes me is that we put up with that guy for years, and when we finally stood our ground with him, it was over in about 10 seconds. Nobody got fired, nobody had to quit over it, he just shut up like a clam. I don't know why we never did it before.

Not all cases of harassment can be resolved so easily, but you can often find allies once you break the chain of silence and start talking about your situation.

Now you're ready to take the next step: speaking with someone who can help you within the company.

Telling Someone in Authority

When a sexual harassment situation calls for a Final Rebuff, it makes sense to involve someone who's in a position of responsibility within the organization. Even if you're not prepared to file a formal complaint immediately, just telling someone in authority can be reassuring, and it may also protect you from any backlash later on if you do decide to formally file a complaint against your harasser.

Talking To Your Boss

Most company policy manuals urge employees with any kind of problem to go directly to the immediate supervisor for help. This is called following the chain of command, and it's usually the recommended course of action. Unfortunately, however, more than 50% of all sexual harassment cases involve a person being harassed by a direct supervisor. If this is true for you, you'll have to find someone else in authority to tell about your situation.

Many organizations provide an alternate channel for employees to talk about sensitive issues or problems other than through the immediate supervisor. They may designate someone in the human resources or personnel area. Some companies refer these cases to an outside counseling service or to their EAP (Employee Assistance Program).

If your employer does not provide these options, and if you can't talk to your direct supervisor, then you should choose the highest level person you can comfortably approach. Choose someone you know is in a position of authority or responsibility.

Enlisting Someone With Power on Your Side

One of the best reasons for telling someone with authority about your situation is that it can provide you with valuable information you'll need to know in advance before taking action. There's a lot at risk when you report someone for sexual harassment, so it's sensible to be cautious, and listen to advice from someone who knows how these things are handled in your company. Once you've found the right person, you should carefully consider how you want to present your story. You'll enhance your credibility if you follow these guidelines:

Explain the Situation Chronologically.

Practice telling your story so you can give the dates, times and details in logical order, as they occurred. The more organized and logical you seem, the more credible you will appear. Jumping from one incident to another, out of sequence, or adding extraneous details can be confusing. You may sound as if you're being selective about what actually happened.

Be Specific and State the Facts.

Describe the behavior, giving specific details about what was said, what was done, and your response. Be direct and honest. Don't equivocate and don't try to offer reasons or excuses for why it happened. Getting diverted into a debate about your harasser's real intentions gets you nowhere. Why it happened is not what concerns you; getting the behavior to stop is what's important.

Show that You Know the Legal Definition of Sexual Harassment.

Let your listener know that you understand the legal criteria for sexual harassment and explain why you believe your situation fits that criteria. You'll give the impression that you are serious and well-informed, instead of just reacting emotionally to an isolated incident. Again, getting into discussions of what is or what isn't sexual harassment are counterproductive. Use the Four-Question Reality Check (see page 5) as your "outline" in defining why you believe this is sexual harassment.

Confirm that You Have Documentation.

Your written record enhances your credibility. At this point, I'd advise just mentioning that you have documented the situation, instead of showing it or handing it in to the company representative. It's far too volatile a document—and too valuable to your case—to treat it lightly. Letting your listener know that you've kept a record of what's happened shows you are serious about getting it stopped.

Keep Your Emotions in Control.

It takes courage to talk about sexual harassment with another person, especially someone you may not know well or someone who holds a position of authority at your company. If you can control your emotions, however, you'll appear much more credible. You'll give the impression that you know what's fair and aren't so upset that you won't be able to assist in getting the situation resolved. Practicing what you want to say beforehand can really help.

Ask for Assistance.

After you've carefully outlined what happened, ask for the individual's assistance. This practical approach not only enhances your credibility, it also positions you as being reasonable and cooperative. It's much better than telling your story and then threatening to take matters into your own hands. That sounds like a threat, and it's not something company representatives

135

want to hear. It can make them defensive and less likely to support you.

Explain what your expectations are—usually that you want the harassment to stop—and when you expect something to be done. Ask for advice on how you can resolve the situation without having to file a formal complaint or involve someone from the outside.

One of the things employers fear most is that employees with complaints will become so angry and frustrated over a situation that they'll seek legal advice or go outside for help without informing the company first. Your willingness to cooperate and to save everyone from embarassment or possible negative publicity should be appreciated by your company and should enhance your credibility.

The memorandum on the following page is an example of an organized way to make such a presentation. It's in memo form here, but you could adapt it as a script to practice presenting your own situation.

MEMORANDUM

DATE:
TO: Company Representative
FROM: Your Name
SUBJECT: Sexual Harassment

I want to discuss a situation that is very upsetting to me. It involves Mr. Roberts, my supervisor. He is sexually harassing me. I don't like it, and I have asked him to stop, but he won't. This situation is seriously affecting how I do my job and how I feel about working here.

On a Wednesday morning two weeks ago (give specific date), Mr. Roberts approached me in the hallway and made a comment about my dress. He said, "I really like the way you look in that dynamite dress." I took it as a compliment, but it made me a little uncomfortable when he kept repeating that all day long. I decided to just let it pass. I like Mr. Roberts and enjoy working with him, but the things he was saying and the way he said it just wasn't really right to be saying at the office. They were very personal things, and I was embarrassed.

Then last Friday morning (give specific date), he came up to me in the parking lot as I was coming to work and said, "You've got that sexy red dress on again... the one that really turns me on. You know what it can do to my whole day when I see you walk in with that on? It gets so bad, all I can think of is taking that dress off you so I can get some real work done."

Page 1

I was very embarrassed. I told him to stop saying things like that to me, that they made me feel very uncomfortable and they weren't appropriate. He just sort of laughed and gave me a look that really upset me. I spent 20 minutes in the ladies' room trying to calm down so I could go to work. Then when he said something again to me later that day, I started keeping notes about what he was saying and doing. I have this written report at home.

The situation has gotten worse. Every time I pass him in the hall or walk past his office, he makes a comment to me about my body and how much I turn him on. This morning, he came up behind me in the hall outside the lunch room and put his arm around me. When I tried to get away from him, he held me against him very close and repeated some of the sexual remarks he had said to me earlier. Other people saw it, but I don't think they knew what was going on. I got away from him as fast as I could.

This thing is making it very hard for me to do my job. I can't concentrate and I dread seeing him. What he is doing to me is sexual harassment and I want it to stop. What can you do to help me get him to stop?

Your Signature

Dealing with Denial, Avoidance, and Disbelief

Despite your best efforts, you may find that the individual you tell chooses not to believe you. This is more often a business decision, rather than a personal decision, but it doesn't make it any easier for you to accept.

Sexual harassment is a very serious charge. Companies are aware of how such a charge can undermine them financially, as well as affect morale and employee productivity. If the person you tell is in a position of responsibility within the company, his or her primary management objective will be to protect the interests and liability of the organization. This doesn't necessarily mean that the company won't be compassionate and concerned about your situation, but you need to be realistic about where their primary interests lie.

If this happens to you, don't give up. You may find someone else in the company who is willing to help you, or you may decide that the company is not going to be cooperative in doing something about the harassment. Document what happened in your first meeting and include this with your other documentation. If you later decide to file a complaint, it'll be helpful to show the good-faith effort you made to resolve the situation.

Supporting Others and Ourselves

Some women perceive their female co-workers or other women in the workplace as non-supportive and prefer to go it alone, rather than rely on others for support. I find this tragic. We need each other. Our

139

numbers in leadership positions are still far too small, and we face so many challenges. No matter how competitive the workplace becomes, there is always a need to show concern and support for others. Alone, our voices depend heavily on our personal courage. In unity, there is tremendous strength.

Susan's Story
Age 34, Defense Industry Technician

I knew who Ellen was, but I'd never really talked to her. She was the first woman manager in this division, and the story on her was that she got her job by destroying her competition. She was one tough cookie. I always kind of held her in awe. It never would have occurred to me in a million years to talk to her about my sexual harassment situation.

One day, I was in the ladies' room and talking to a friend of mine about the latest episode I had with my boss. I looked up and there was Ellen, staring at me in the mirror.

I looked into the eyes of this smart, tough woman and I knew she knew exactly what I was talking about. I stared back at her and whispered, "You know what I mean?" She was quiet for a moment and then she stared right back at me and said, "Do I ever! What's the jerk's name?"

I can't tell you what a difference it made to have her on my side. He got called on the carpet so fast, it made his head spin. Eventually, he was fired. I don't care what people say about Ellen, she really went to bat for me, and I know it was because she'd been there before herself.

Chapter 14

FILING A FORMAL COMPLAINT WITH YOUR EMPLOYER

Keeping It on the Inside Track

Y ou may be so angry and frustrated over your harasser's persistence, that filing a formal complaint against him may seem like the only option you have that can make him stop. It's an option, however, that can also hold risks for you.

Officially reporting a case of sexual harassment can be a very positive action, but you'll want to proceed carefully each step of the way. In this chapter, you'll learn how to assess the risks involved, how to safeguard against backlash, and how to present your case in the most effective way possible.

As I've said earlier, a company is required by law to maintain a workplace free of sexual harassment. Some employers take this responsibility seriously. But the issues surrounding sexual harassment are so complex, and the financial and legal liability so broad, that few companies are equipped to really deal with it effectively. Depending upon your company's commitment to resolving the issue fairly, the formal complaint process can be empowering—or it can be a nightmare.

Where Does Your Company Stand?

If your company doesn't have a formal policy on sexual harassment, you're not alone. Despite the fact that over 80% of the Fortune 500 companies claim to have a policy and training program in place, less than half of the readers responding to *Working Woman's* 1992 survey say they work for a company that has them.[1]

The two groups were even more divided on the issue of how complaints about sexual harassment were handled. The company representatives surveyed claimed that over 80% of offenders[2] who were reported were punished justly by the company, while only 21% of the workers agreed.

Should You Report Your Situation?

For some women, the complaint process can be a positive one. This was the case for Angela.

Angela's Story
Age 28, Consumer Relations Specialist

I agonized about reporting the situation. I worried about losing my job, and I'd heard a lot of people say that the company wasn't that sympathetic to employee complaints. I felt like I was taking a big risk.

It took me a long time to work up my courage, but I am so glad I finally did it. The

---

1. "Sexual Harassment in the Fortune 500," *Working Woman,* 1992.
2. This figure was down from 90% in the initial survey taken in 1988 by *Working Woman.*

people in human resources were very supportive and professional about it. They never made me feel that they didn't believe me. Of course, I found out later that I wasn't the first one to come forward with the same complaint. Apparently, they'd been watching my boss for months because of rumors about him, but no one had ever filed an official complaint about him.

The company investigated the situation and he got fired. Some people may think I was a trouble maker, but I don't care. I feel like I did something good for the rest of the women who work here. And getting him out of my life was worth it.

Other women say they regret their decision to file a complaint. Consider JoAnne's story:

JoAnne's Story, Age 33, Sales Representative

Believe me, if I could do it over again, I would keep my mouth shut. I went to the human resources manager because my boss was becoming so abusive to me that I couldn't see any other way to handle it. I couldn't quit, and it made me furious that he could just get away with that stuff. He even went so far as to call me at home and leave heavy breathing messages on my phone. I knew it was him, because the next day he always asked me if I'd had any interesting messages I wanted to talk to him about. He followed me everywhere, even to the bathroom. It was really sickening.

When I reported him, the company acted like I was accusing this guy of grand larceny or something. They flew me over to corporate headquarters and I got grilled by about six different people—really the third degree, like I was on trial. They told me that if I carried this thing any further, it would cost both of us our jobs. I didn't have to think twice. I dropped the whole thing.

The Realities of Reporting

Even if your company appears to take a strong stand against sexual harassment, the company representatives won't be pleased to find out it's happening. The realities of reporting sexual harassment aren't usually found in the pages of the policy manual, however well-intentioned that policy might appear.

Often victims are shocked to discover that previously friendly or supportive staff people may suddenly back away or shun them after a sexual harassment complaint has been filed. Don't expect company representatives to accept without question what you have to report. They'll want to investigate the situation and plan what they are going to do about it. You must remember that your employer's number-one concern in sexual harassment cases is liability.

Don't expect the strong relationships you may have forged with your boss, your co-workers, or the powers at the head office to protect you either. Those ties can be strained if the company feels threatened by a lawsuit or the messy publicity of a harassment scandal. You may have your champions and admirers, but be aware that sexual harassment tests loyalties and disrupts even the best relationships.

Be alert to the "political" winds. If your harasser is a powerful or prominent member of the organization, or if his position is much higher than yours, you'll want to find out as much as you can about how your company may have resolved a similar situation in the past. Don't let office politics alone dictate your course of action, but be aware of the realities you could face.

Before you make your decision, here are some questions to consider about your company's commitment on preventing sexual harassment:

- Does your company have a formal policy on sexual harassment?

- Does the company seem sincere in its commitment to employee issues such as equal opportunity and equal treatment?

- Does the company handle personnel matters with confidentiality, or does the whole office know if someone makes a complaint, puts in for personal leave, or asks for a raise?

- Does there seem to be a "double standard" of behavior, morals, or professionalism for executives and for "the rest of us?" Is that standard the same for men and for women?

- Is there a procedure for complaints about sensitive issues that also includes alternatives, other than reporting to your direct supervisor?

- Is there an "open door" policy at your company for employees? Does the door really stay open, or is it considered poor judgment to discuss private concerns like sexual harassment with your boss or with management?

Answering these questions objectively may give you some idea of what to expect from your company if you decide to file a formal complaint. A trustworthy co-worker, who is savvy about the inner workings of the company, may also be able to give you some help.

The Realities of Retaliation

When you're preparing to report sexual harassment, there's also the issue of retaliation to consider. You may be the hardest working member of your department or division, the creator of this year's award-winning packaging idea, or the star of the company softball team, but you are first and foremost an employee of your organization. Don't fall into the trap of believing you are indispensable or that your contributions isolate you from retaliation when you report sexual harassment.

What form can that retaliation take?

- Extremely close scrutiny of your job performance and past employment history.
- Negative reports about you to management or co-workers.
- Altered personnel records or "after-the-fact" documentation.
- Reduction in responsibilities or authority.
- Isolation and silence.
- Threats of suspension or termination.

These are strong measures to use against you, but remember that you have three very powerful allies to protect you from retaliation: the laws against sexual harassment, your determination to stand up for your rights, and the documentation record you've continued to keep throughout your ordeal.

Don't base your decision about whether to report sexual harassment on irrational fears or heightened emotions that can cloud your judgment. Harassers frequently make threats about what they'll do to your career or what the company will do to you if you take steps to expose them or their behavior. These threats can be very intimidating, even when you recognize them as further attempts to control and manipulate the situation to your harasser's advantage.

To assess the real consequences of reporting sexual harassment, consider the pros and cons of your present situation at work, including the relationship with your harasser. Then be realistic about how each element affects your job and your career plans.

You might also want to consult someone else to help you assess the situation. For example, **9to5**, The National Association of Working Women, offers advice based on years of counseling victims of workplace harassment. Their toll-free hotline number is: **1-800-522-0925**. They also sponsor local chapters of their organization. A support group like **9to5** can help you gain some new perspectives on reporting your situation, and can also offer you suggestions about other options.

Retaliation is Risky for Everyone

Retaliation may be an effective threat against some victims, but you should realize that it's a very risky proposition for your harasser or your employer. Courts come down hard on companies that retaliate against victims seeking protection from sexual harassment. In many cases, significantly higher awards for damages are determined by the degree of retaliation a victim suffers as a result of reporting it.

As frightening as the prospect of retaliation seems, you do have ways to seek recourse. Your best defense is to keep very careful documentation and try to enlist witnesses. It isn't easy to withstand such treatment, but the alternative—saying or doing nothing to stop the harassment—could be even more devastating to your health, your emotional well-being, and to your future career.

The Smart Way to Report Sexual Harassment

Once you've assessed the risks and decided that it's to your advantage to file a formal complaint with your employer, here's how to make the process work for you. The **seven steps** outlined below will take you from the preparatory steps all the way through the follow-up of your report.

1. Safeguard Your Employee Records Before You Proceed

If you're going to file a formal complaint, there's one critical step you can't afford to neglect. Before you do anything else, request a copy of your work record from your employer.

Why is this so important? Your work record reflects your history with the company from the date you were hired. Virtually every company keeps records on its employees. Employers have the right to include anything in the file they feel is pertinent about you as an employee, including: performance appraisals, salary

148

history and payroll information, disciplinary actions or reports, commendations or awards, and other confidential information about you.

Altering work records is a big temptation for many companies faced with a formal complaint about sexual harassment, especially when they fear an extensive investigation or an expensive legal battle. The only way you'll know if your file has been altered is to be able to compare it to the records you've requested before you filed a complaint. *You have a right to have access to this information.*

Work records are one of the first things subpoenaed from your employer in any legal action or outside investigation about sexual harassment. It's to your advantage to know the contents of your personnel records before you make an official complaint.

If you can make a copy, get a notary to date it for you. If company regulations prohibit making copies of the file's contents, ask to see the information and then make your own list of what it contains.

2. Find Out How Your Company Wants You to Proceed

As I've suggested earlier, find out what your company's requirements are for reporting sexual harassment before you talk to someone. If your company has established such guidelines or procedures, you're likely to find them detailed in your employee manual, or posted in a common-use area.

Organizations that have established complaint procedures usually expect you to follow them. Ask if your company has an Equal Employment Opportunity officer, or someone who's been appointed to handle such complaints. Many companies also advise managers on how to assist employees in the complaint process.

Some organizations provide several options for reporting sexual harassment, such as written complaint forms or confidential interviews with an ombudsman, Employee Assistance Program (EAP), or employee relations specialist. If you belong to a union, there's usually a formal grievance procedure for you to follow.

Once you've chosen the approach that seems most reasonable to you, be sure to follow your company's guidelines exactly. This is important for two reasons: it will insure that your complaint is heard by the right person, and it will strengthen your position should you later decide to take your complaint outside the company.

Don't allow a technicality in the reporting process to derail the focus of your complaint. You want the company to intervene in a situation you find intolerable. Wasting time because you haven't followed procedure can be frustrating. It can put you at a disadvantage with the people who can help you most.

3. Know Your Rights Under the Law

Understanding your rights can give you the courage to exercise them. Local, state and federal governments write laws prohibiting discrimination and sexual harassment, and those laws are to protect you. Learn what they are, and how they apply to your situation.

Most company policies also spell out your rights to make a complaint or file a grievance. If your company has no policy statement on sexual harassment, call the nearest office of the Equal Employment Opportunity

Commission (EEOC),[3] or your state's human rights agency, and request information on the laws governing sexual harassment.

4. Develop a strategy

You'll help yourself tremendously if you plan logically how to make the best use of the company's reporting procedures, and how much time you feel is reasonable for them to investigate and act on your complaint. Writing down your plan and time lines is a helpful way to organize your strategy. Proceeding in a logical and organized way will increase your credibility and give you more confidence.

Now is the time to review the documentation you've kept on your harasser's behavior toward you. Make sure the information is organized chronologically, and that you've included anything that could be considered evidence of the harassment, such as notes, memos, or recordings sent to you by your harasser. Reviewing your documentation will help you be clear and factual in reporting your situation to others.

Don't forget to plan for your own emotional needs, too. You'll find this whole process much easier to face if you have the support of others. Your friends, family members or a professional counselor can help you maintain your determination to gain justice.

5. Plan Carefully What You Want to Say

It's a good idea to write down what you want to say when you report the harassment, as if you're preparing

---

3. For offices see Appendix B for state-by-state listings.

a presentation. You'll need to include the specific details of your situation, how it makes you feel, and what you expect the company to do about it.

6. Consider Your Credibility

We've already discussed the fact that many victims of sexual harassment don't report it because they think they won't be believed. Credibility can be a problem if company officials discredit your report or trivialize sexual harassment as a "private matter between two people."

Most organizations are highly sensitized to the issue of sexual harassment. The chances that they'll dismiss your report out-of-hand are extremely low. In fact, you'll gain credibility (in the eyes of the court) just by making a formal complaint. If your employer is unresponsive and you decide to later take your complaint outside the company, the fact that you reported it and the company did nothing about it will be a key factor in your favor.

Before you meet with a company representative to begin the complaint process, review the information given in Chapter 12, "Enhancing Your Credibility."

7. Follow Up Your Report

When you file a formal complaint about sexual harassment, your employer has an obligation to investigate the situation in a timely manner. The employer's response to an internal employee complaint has legal considerations, too, since the law considers the timeliness of the employer's response to be a key indication of its good faith in resolving the situation. From your point of view, of course, the more quickly the company takes action, the better. But you should also be understanding and reasonable about the time involved to investigate the situation. Here are some guidelines for following up with your employer.

NOTE: At the conclusion of the initial complaint interview, ask specifically what will happen next and how long it will take.

SAY:
Please tell me what happens next. I'd also like to know when I can expect this matter to be resolved.

SAY:
Naturally, I want this matter to be resolved as soon as possible. I would like to check with you next Friday to find out what progress has been made.

Your employer needs time to investigate the situation, and you want to appear cooperative, but it's not unreasonable for you to request a time period for the investigation. You want to resolve the situation and get on with your life as soon as possible. Leaving it open-ended puts you in the position of not knowing what the company intends or how long you'll have to wait for a resolution. That can be frustrating and stressful.

If the person handling your complaint seems unable or unwilling to specify a definite date for you to check back, suggest one yourself.

SAY:
I understand that right now it's hard to know how long it will take. I'd like to check back with you at the end of next

week to see what progress has been made. Will 3:30 on Friday afternoon, (give specific date) be convenient?

Then make sure you mark the date on your calendar and follow up. If there's no progress, or if the person puts you off, be persistent and repeat your request for a resolution date. You might want to put it in writing this time.

Here's an example of a follow-up memo you might consider sending to your employer's representative:

MEMORANDUM

DATE:

TO: (The Investigator or Company Representative)

FROM: (Your full name, title, and department)

SUBJECT: Sexual Harassment Complaint

As we discussed in our meeting of (date), you agreed to begin investigating my complaint of sexual harassment by (name of your harasser).

At that time, you told me I could expect to receive information on the company's findings by (give promised date). I heard nothing from you on that day, and I have been unable to reach you by telephone.

I am writing to request that we meet to discuss this matter on (give specific date). Please confirm if this is convenient, or provide me with an alternate date and time.

Keep copies of any memo you might send, and also make a note of any conversations you have with anyone from the company regarding the investigation. Asking for a resolution date, and following up your report is an assertive way to relieve some of the stress you'll probably feel while an investigation is being made. It gives you a way to measure progress, and it also lets your employer know that you expect results.

Gaining the Courage to Continue

Few issues are more devastating to job security than a claim of sexual harassment against someone who is your supervisor or even a co-worker. The fallout surrounding it can be so great, that just making the decision to file a complaint—even if you are completely right and justified in doing so—can make tremendous demands on you.

Most harassers know quite well how difficult it is for their victims to speak up. They know that few victims ever report harassment, however blatant it might be. Many of them feel immune because of this and because of their position within the company.

Reporting harassment to your employer can be a major step toward stopping it. Reporting it sends a powerful message to your harasser and others that you refuse to be intimidated by behavior that is offensive, unprofessional, and illegal.

The Gossip Machine

Nothing is more titillating to an office full of people than gossip about sex. Co-workers feel few reservations about serving as judge and jury when it comes to a situation involving the volatile mix of sex and power.

The gossip machine is a powerful force in its own right. We all want to be liked and accepted by the people we work with, and the specialized environment of work encourages teamwork and alliances. Many victims choose to remain silent rather than submit themselves to the censure of their co-workers.

It can be difficult to segregate yourself from the group by calling attention to a situation that is both complex and highly personal to you. There's always the possibility that you will be ostracized or criticized by others if you report someone for sexual harassment. Yet often, we're unaware that others may be experiencing similar situations to our own. If you do report it, you may find that others will also come forward to confirm the harassment.

Here are three ideas on how you can deal with gossip:

1. Be aware of appearances.

How others perceive you has a great deal to do with how supportive they may be of your decision to report the harassment. If you feel that an incident or comment has given others the wrong impression, or if you've been compromised by gossip or rumor, deal with it directly. If you can, confront the people you work with, and do it quickly to correct any misinterpretations that could cause you problems later.

2. Be honest about the situation.

If you lie, act mysterious, or in some way attempt to cover up or hide the situation, you may seriously erode your own credibility with others. They usually already know about it or have strong suspicions that something's going on. Avoiding the issue or lying about it can be very self-defeating.

Sometimes saying nothing may seem like your best policy, but it can often lead to misunderstandings. Should you choose to involve others, be honest with them about what's happening to you and how you feel about it. Letting others know you are upset signals that you are not welcoming the attentions of your harasser.

3. Refuse to participate.

If you join in the gossip or rumors about others, you may be signalling that you approve of this behavior, or that you don't find it offensive. Participating in sexual jokes, innuendoes, or similar activities doesn't disqualify you from later reporting sexual harassment, but it can send mixed messages to others, and it can weaken your position with your co-workers and employer.

Chapter 15

USING THE GOVERNMENT AGENCIES

Taking It Outside

I f you can't resolve your sexual harassment complaint to your satisfaction within your company, you can seek outside-help from the appropriate state or federal agency. Agency staff will investigate your complaint, and try to help you and your employer resolve it. If that doesn't work, and the agency staff decides your case has merit, they may even file a lawsuit against the employer on your behalf. The good news is that this won't cost you a thing. The downside is that you may have to wait an extraordinary amount of time for a government agency to act.

The Realities of Bureaucracy

The intent to assist individuals in resolving complaints against those who are depriving them of their rights is ostensibly why federal agencies like the Equal Employment Opportunity Commission (EEOC) exist.

If things worked as they were intended, you could complete a simple application form, have your case assigned to a sympathetic case worker experienced in dealing with sexual harassment complaints, and have your complaint skillfully and efficiently investigated and resolved through conciliation. If conciliation failed, the agency would then be ready to represent you in litigation against your employer. Unfortunately, it rarely works this way.

Every state except Alabama, Arkansas, Georgia, Louisiana and Mississippi include Fair Employment Practices in their employment laws. Agencies are set up to investigate and handle complaints. These agencies, like government bureaucracies everywhere, are chronically understaffed and burdened with an appalling backlog of cases. Sometimes, it seems the bureaucracy itself is ineffective.

Understanding Your Options

You have two options when you take your complaint to a government agency for redress. You can file your complaint under the United States Civil Rights Act with the Equal Employment Opportunity Commission (EEOC),[1] or you can file under a similar state law with a Fair Employment Practices (FEP) agency.[2]

State agencies often have less restrictive filing requirements. They may also have less of a backlog than the EEOC and may be able to offer you easier access to the information you need. Always check first

---

1. Certain restrictions may apply. If your company has less than the EEOC minimum of 15 employees, you may need to file through a state agency. Check with the EEOC office nearest you to be sure.
2. Government employees must file through the EEOC under separate procedures. Always check first to find what procedures apply to your personal situation.

before you make a decision about where to file. Find out what exact procedures are required.

Before You Decide to File a Complaint:

1. Call first.

Antidiscrimination agencies are found under the government listings in the telephone directory. Find out where the agencies are located and if they require an appointment.

2. Ask for the latest updates on laws regarding sexual harassment in your state.[3]

When you receive the information, read it carefully. If there is something you don't understand, call and ask someone at the agency to explain it to you.

3. Confirm the filing procedures.

Ask for copies of the most current filing forms and specific information on how to file a complaint. There is no margin for error when you are dealing with a government agency, and you don't want your complaint delayed or dismissed on a technicality. Also ask who will be handling each phase of the procedure. Having a person's name can help you cut through some of the delays you may encounter, even if all that person does is to refer you to someone else.

---

3. If you request information to be sent to you directly, be sure to ask when you can expect it. Since backlogs are common, you may ask for an alternative way to receive the information more promptly. You may also be able to find this information in your public library.

4. Confirm time limitations and requirements.

Find out the exact filing deadlines, including the time limits and restrictions on filing complaints. This is an extremely important thing for you to know because time limits and statutes of limitations may be interpreted differently from one state to another. If you aren't sure, ask for clarification.

When you file has a great deal of bearing on your case. You'll undoubtedly want to give your employer adequate time to resolve your sexual harassment complaint before you look for help from a government agency. Don't delay too long however. If you don't file within a specified period of time, you could become ineligible to have your case investigated.

Although the EEOC requires you to file a complaint within 180 days of an incident of sexual harassment, some states will allow you only up to 65 days before the statute of limitations expires. If you file with your state agency, find out exactly what time restrictions apply. (See Appendix C.) Be sure to double-check to make sure the time limits in your state haven't changed or been adjusted by more recent legislation.

Also ask how the agency in your state interprets the filing period. If the agency "starts the clock" with the first sexual harassment incident, you may have to make decisions more quickly, since the clock may have started. When you first reported the situation to your employer may have been much later. If the harassment took place over a period of weeks or months, this could significantly affect the amount of time you have to file a formal complaint.

5. Ask how long it takes for the agency to review your case and make a determination about it.

Again, you must check first to find out the exact procedures that apply in your state. Your state agency will usually be able to give you an estimate of how long the complaint procedure takes, but it could possibly take longer than the estimate.

If you file under EEOC requirements, once the formal complaint is drawn, it is sent to the employer within ten working days. The employer then has 30 days to respond, but extensions are common. This can be an especially stressful time for you—especially if you remain on your job while the complaint is filed. Be prepared for delays. Most employers seek legal counsel immediately upon receiving a formal complaint notice from the EEOC, and lawyers are usually very skilled at obtaining additional time for their clients to respond. The EEOC usually grants the additional time requested for the employer to investigate the situation, because the EEOC is interested in resolving the complaint without further action and expense.

What About Retaliation?

Delays are one thing, but retaliation against you for standing up for your rights is illegal, as is the alteration or destruction of documentation pertinent to the charge. If you remain on the job while your complaint is being investigated by an outside agency, and if your employer retaliates against you in any way, you should document the situation and report it immediately to the EEOC.

If your employer doesn't cooperate with the initial request, the EEOC can issue a subpoena for information pertaining to your case. Few employers will risk the stiff penalties or a charge of noncompliance with the EEOC by ignoring a subpoena. However, obtaining a subpoena order takes time, and additional time is required for a response.

What Comes Next?

After the employer submits a response, the EEOC will usually schedule a conference or pre-investigation meeting. This is not a formal hearing on the case. No judge is involved. The purpose of this meeting is to seek agreement between the two parties (you and your employer) to resolve the complaint if possible.

Both parties are asked to attend, as well as the EEOC investigators assigned to the case, any witnesses you have named in your complaint, and legal counselors or other such representatives. The EEOC will ask both sides to respond to the charge. This meeting will determine whether or not the agency will proceed with a full investigation of the situation. How long it takes to schedule this conference depends on the EEOC's backlog of cases, the availability of all parties, and enough other factors to delay this step by weeks or months.

The Investigation Process

If the EEOC determines that agreement cannot be reached, the representative may instigate a full investigation of the complaint. This means they will interview witnesses, visit the work site, and gather information necessary for them to make a determination of the evidence. They are trying to decide if the charge of sexual harassment has merit.

163

During this phase, which can also take days, weeks or months, both sides will be asked to supply the EEOC with documentation to represent their side of the case. Here is where your documentation journal will play a crucial role in helping the EEOC investigator determine the merits of your case. Be aware that your employer will also submit information, including testimony from witnesses, in an attempt to disprove your allegations.

Once the investigation is completed, the EEOC will issue a formal determination of its findings. The agency representitives will notify both parties, who can then request a review of the findings.

The EEOC Determination

If the EEOC determines that there is no reasonable cause for your complaint under their guidelines, they will give you a Right-to-Sue letter which will allow you to take the matter to court in a private lawsuit if you wish.[4]

A finding of "no reasonable cause" by the EEOC *is not necessarily an end to the matter,* or an indication that what you experienced isn't sexual harassment. EEOC standards are very strict. Demands on the federal agency are high, not only because of reduced personnel and lack of funding available to litigate cases, but also because of politics. You may find that state agencies are less stringent than federal offices in cause determinations.

---

4.   You can request a "Right-to-Sue" letter from the EEOC after 180 days have elapsed, regardless of where you are in the EEOC complaint process. Once you have initiated an EEOC complaint, you cannot file a private lawsuit without this letter.

Conciliation or Court?

Should the EEOC find that there is reasonable cause for your discrimination complaint, they have two options: 1) conciliation or 2) litigation. To resolve the matter through a process called conciliation means the EEOC will ask the employer to take steps to stop the discrimination and offer you an acceptable remedy. This might mean a transfer to another job or location, termination or disciplinary action taken against your harasser, a financial settlement, or another arrangement that you may find agreeable.

On rare occasions, the EEOC will select their second option and have their lawyers *litigate* on your behalf. This happens in less than 1 percent of cases submitted to the EEOC. Even if the EEOC determines that litigation is an option they will consider, the backlogs and bureaucracy can be so daunting that you may choose instead to hire an attorney and pursue a private lawsuit on your own. The Right-to-Sue letter allows you to do that.

If your case does go to litigation, everything starts over from the beginning. There will be an investigative period, requests and subpoenas for relevant information, and additional time needed by the legal representatives to prepare the case. The EEOC determination may or may not be admissible in court. Either way, you should expect additional delays of months, perhaps years, before the case is heard.

Is It Worth the Effort?

It's easy to become discouraged when you learn about the huge backlogs of cases and the amount of

165

paperwork necessary to pursue a sexual harassment complaint. Dealing with government institutions is rarely without its challenges to your patience and perseverance, but there are benefits to using these resources to help you solve your problem.

Strong Laws and Strong Remedies

After over a decade of disappointing rulings and questionable interpretations, the emphasis seems to be shifting toward better protection for victims of sexual harassment. This has been particularly true since new amendments to the Civil Rights Act were passed in 1991, allowing individuals who file actions under the law to collect up to $300,000 in compensatory and punitive damages. Many states have also tightened their laws on sexual harassment and added measures to protect victims from retaliation and emotional distress.

The attention focused on the issue of sexual harassment during the Clarence Thomas hearings has also had an impact. Women in particular, were outraged at the treatment Anita Hill received from the Senate Judiciary committee. This anger has been heard by elected officials and those seeking public office.

Newspaper stories and articles, printed in a broad range of publications, have continued to keep the issue in the public light. People's perceptions of what role government should play in preventing sexual harassment are changing. Expectations can put pressure on government agencies like the EEOC to do a better job of responding to the needs of complainants.

Power and Perception

The EEOC and state agencies may appear to be mired in their own complexities, but you shouldn't underestimate the power they hold over employers. Battling a government agency over anything is a nightmare for most businesses, and when the fight involves the negative publicity that often surrounds discrimination cases, most employers have even more reason to want to avoid a confrontation. That's why the EEOC is often successful in bringing about conciliation between victims and their employers, before a formal investigation starts. These cases don't often garner the attention of legal battles or huge financial awards, but they are victories in their own right.

There also seems to be a growing emphasis on the social responsibility of employers. The perception of an employer who offers a discrimination-free workplace is a positive one. Increasingly, corporations and institutions are mindful of the image they portray to employees and the communities they serve.

Shifts in Staffing and Attitudes

Although inadequate funding and cutbacks in personnel have had an impact on all government agencies, it's possible to find responsive staff representatives at the EEOC and state agencies who handle sexual harassment complaints. The irony that Clarence Thomas served as head of the EEOC during the period in which he allegedly harassed Anita Hill has not escaped the public's attention, and neither has the government's own problems with sexual harassment. Consequently, there's been a new emphasis on training. Better trained staff and administrators are less likely to be rude, or to give you incomplete or misleading information.

The Big Advantage Is Cost

Because the EEOC and state agencies exist to serve the public, it's possible to resolve a sexual harassment problem without hiring your own attorney or incurring huge costs for litigation. Legal costs of pursuing a sexual harassment case can run well over $100,000 or more. This fact alone can make the EEOC or related state agencies a more reasonable alternative for you.

Many professional organizations and special interest groups offer counseling services that can help you determine the legal merits of a discrimination case. They can help you evaluate whether or not your case would best be served by a government agency or by hiring a private attorney. These services are sometimes free or have very minimal fees. A listing of organizations you might contact for these services appears in Appendix A.

How to Help Yourself

If you've decided to file a complaint with a government agency, give yourself every advantage by following these simple guidelines.

1. Stay on top of things.

Filing a formal complaint is a complex process, and it's easy to let little details slip by. Don't risk jeopardizing your own case by being disorganized. Get a three-ring binder and keep everything related to your claim in one place. Include a calendar with space to make notes, and be sure to keep track of deadlines and when things have been promised to you.

Make copies of all the forms you complete and make a note at the top when you submitted the completed form and the name of the person and agency to whom it was submitted. Keep receipts for insured or certified postage here, too.

2. Stay active and informed.

Don't expect to complete a complaint form and then leave everything else to the agency. Know the laws that govern your situation and how they can protect you. Follow directions and filing procedures to the letter. If you don't understand something, ask. If you still don't understand, ask again or find someone else who can answer your question satisfactorily.

Be cooperative, and provide as much information as you can in as timely a manner as possible. Taking an active role in your own case will keep you informed and will also help agency representatives do their job better.

3. Stay assertive.

Remember that the agency handling your complaint exists to serve you. You have a right to expect that the agency representatives treat you in a courteous and professional manner and take appropriate action on your behalf. Keep a list of all the people who assist you, including their titles and their areas of responsibility.

State your requests in positive and cooperative terms, but be assertive about what you expect them to do for you. Ask for everything you are entitled to under the law, including specifics such as reinstatement

169

to your position, back pay, health care expenses, legal fees, and any financial compensation allowed by law.

If the agency representatives promise you action by a certain date, follow up with the person to make sure it is done. If it isn't, you have the right to speak to someone else, higher in authority, who can help you.

4. Keep your options open.

Using the resources of the EEOC or a state agency doesn't mean you are committed to staying with them. If you feel the backlogs are too excessive or that your interests are not being well represented, you can opt to cancel your complaint, request a Right-to-Sue letter, and seek help in the private sector.

On the other hand, you should be open to suggestions given to you by experienced agency representatives. They may be able to help you negotiate a conciliation with your employer that you thought was impossible to accomplish.

Is this Option the Right Choice for You?

Making the decision to file a complaint of sexual harassment with an outside agency takes a tremendous amount of courage. That courage can continue to be tested by the labyrinth of bureaucratic maneuverings and red tape involved in taking a complaint to resolution. Those who have the fortitude and patience to stay with the process help all of us gain confidence in a system that should serve us. For some of us, however, allowing the process to drag on for months or years is more than we can bear.

If you feel that you have explored your options with the EEOC or a state agency, and have found them too restrictive or too frustrating for your needs, you may find that taking private legal action against your employer is well worth the expense. The next chapter offers the pros and cons of taking your case to court and advice on how to find the right attorney to represent you.

Chapter 16

NAVIGATING THE LEGAL LABYRINTH

Filing a Lawsuit

A good attorney can be one of your best allies in your fight against a company that has failed to safeguard your rights. In this chapter, you'll learn how to choose an attorney who can make the legal system work for you.

What Do You Want?

One of the first things an attorney will ask you when you give an overview of your situation is: *What do you want out of this?* Do you want back wages, punitive damages, reinstatement, revenge? This is a question you need to consider carefully. You'll save yourself time and money if you know what you want before you seek legal advice.

How to Find An Attorney

Most people ask friends and relatives to recommend a lawyer when they need one. With sexual harassment cases, you want to be sure the person you hire to represent you is experienced with discrimination cases. Not every attorney is.

If you want a quality referral, consider calling local women's business organizations and professional leagues, a women's support group at the local university, or the local chapter of a national women's organization like **9to5** or the National Organization of Women (NOW). Ask them if they know which attorneys in your area specialize in women's issues, and ask who has been most successful in representing sexual harassment plaintiffs.

This is far better than simply calling the local bar association, or a lawyer referral service. Often these services only carry lists of attorneys by specialty; they don't have performance standards and they don't make specific recommendations.

How to Interview An Attorney

Once you have a few names, start by making some phone calls. There are three basic questions you should ask a prospective attorney:

1. What is your background in representing sexual harassment cases?

Find out how many cases the attorney has represented for plaintiffs like yourself. (As the plaintiff, you are the person bringing legal action against someone else. In this case, your harasser and/or your employer become the defendants.) Often attorneys who specialize in employment law have more practice defending employers than individual plaintiffs. You need to know this in advance.

Also ask the attorney how recently she or he has handled cases. The laws on sexual harassment have changed in the last ten years, and they continue to do

173

so. Be sure to ask the attorney how many cases she has tried, similar to yours, and how many of these she has won. Each case is different, of course, but a win/loss record is still pertinent, so ask about it.

2. What are your fees, and is there a charge for an initial consultation?

The biggest source of problems between attorneys and clients usually involves misunderstandings about fees. Legal action is expensive. Any attorney's livelihood is based on the fees he/she generates. Few can afford to donate the time and money required for a case like this, however sympathetic they may be. Don't be shy about asking up front how much it will cost.

Find out if the attorney will take a case like yours on an hourly fee basis or on contingency. There's a big difference. You can expect to pay from $75 to $300 per hour for the services of an attorney, and that includes every single phone call, letter, search for information, or deposition performed on your behalf.

Most attorneys, who accept cases on contingency, base their percentage on the length of the case. If they can settle the case for you early in the process, before a lawsuit is filed, they may require a fee of 25 to 35 percent of the settlement. If a lawsuit is filed through the courts, even if it gets settled before the trial, the fee may be 35 to 40 percent. The fee can be as high as 50 percent of your award, if the case is tried before a jury.

Don't be discouraged by the expense. Many sexual harassment laws include provisions to reclaim your attorney's costs—if you win. Remember that contingency agreements represent a risk for your attorney, too. If you lose the case, your attorney loses everything invested in trying the case.

Get the fee agreement with your attorney in writing before you proceed. This can be a simple letter stating that you are hiring the attorney to pursue your case as of this date, for this specified fee. And, if you don't understand something about fees, be sure to ask in advance.

3. Do you have time for this case?

It may seem like an obvious question, but it's a valid one, especially if you plan to stay at your job while you proceed with a lawsuit. You should expect your attorney to be able to devote a reasonable amount of time to working with you on the development of your case. If the attorney's case load is too busy, find someone else to take your case. Don't hire an attorney who promises to "fit you in" an already crowded schedule, or who asks you to wait weeks before even meeting with you for the first consultation.

This is particularly important if you are still at your job. "Once you initiate a lawsuit against your employer, you sever any opportunity for a positive relationship," says Conni L. Stamper, an attorney who has represented both plaintiffs and defendants in employment discrimination cases. "If you keep your job, the work environment will definitely be altered."[1]

---

1.   Stamper, Conni L. Interview with author. Spokane, WA, 1992.

Have Realistic Expectations

Don't expect an attorney to make an instant assessment of the merit of your case on the phone. A competent professional needs to hear your story in detail. An attorney needs to judge several important factors, such as the amount of documentation or other evidence you have, and what kind of witness you'll be. These are the fine points of practicing law. An attorney who makes a quick judgment based on a limited telephone conversation is not being fair to you or to your case.

Don't convince yourself your case is unbeatable by trying to be your own lawyer or listening to friends. It's easy to feel as if you're familiar with the legal system from what you see on television or read in the newspaper. Sexual harassment cases do get a lot of publicity, but they are also often highly sensationalized. There's no substitute for sound legal advice based on extensive professional experience. Your attorney will welcome your willingness to help build the strongest case possible.

How Attorneys Assess Clients and Cases (and Why They Refuse Cases)

Attorneys don't practice law to lose cases. Any attorney you hire will want to make sure your case is strong, and that there's a high probability you can prevail against the defendant. The attorney will listen carefully to your story, and will ask you some pertinent questions to confirm his or her assessment of the strength of your case.

Any attorney might seek the anwers to questions, such as the following ones, before deciding whether or

176

not to take a case. Attorneys reject cases for various reasons:

1. The merits of the case don't justify pursuing it.

Is the situation you've described really sexual harassment under local, state, or federal laws? Are there gray areas that would be hard to prove? Is a strong defense of the sexual harassment based on your past history with the employer? Have you had job performance or disciplinary problems before? Does the employer have a history of a strong and well-publicized policy against sexual harassment?

2. There is a lack of evidence to prove sexual harassment.

Is there good documentation showing the chronology of the situation? How long has it been going on? What steps did you take to stop it yourself? Whom did you tell? Did you ask officials of your company to intervene on your behalf, or did you keep the situation to yourself? Did you follow existing policies in reporting the situation?

3. Lack of sympathy toward you as a plaintiff.

Are you of good character? Do you appear honest? Are you "too much" of a victim to be credible to a jury? Do you have a grudge to settle that extends beyond the sexual harassment charge? Are you an employee with problems or are you a problem employee? Are you so emotionally distraught that you need professional help from health care professionals? Will you be strong enough to endure the demands and rigors of a lawsuit?

4. Sexual harassment lawsuits are difficult to win.
The circumstances surrounding sexual harassment are seldom black-and-white. Often, there is little concrete evidence to prove that things happened as the victim says they did.

5. These cases are extremely expensive.
Aside from your attorney's professional time, it takes many hours of support services to prepare a sexual harassment case for trial. Expert testimony alone can cost thousands of dollars. For some attorneys, the up-front costs are too high to make it worthwhile, especially given the fact that so many of these cases are taken on contingency. A typical sexual harassment case can take up to a year to prepare and a year or more to come to trial.

6. The other side is too powerful.
Even if you meet an attorney's criteria for a good plaintiff, he or she may still be reluctant to take your case of sexual harassment because of the defendant, such as a prominent member of the local business community. Huge corporations, as defendants, have strong resources to fight charges of sexual harassment with attorneys on staff. Those who have the resources may maneuver to postpone litigation for such a long period, that the time and expense involved in fighting them is overwhelming.

These are the realities. They don't have to discourage you. Only you can decide if you are willing to risk—and endure—the legal system to gain vindication for the losses you have suffered. The individuals who have won large awards once started out where you may be now—by convincing an attorney to take the case.

What Your Attorney Needs to Know

Once you find a lawyer, you can save the attorney's time and your money by coming to your first meeting armed with all the information he or she is likely to want. Be sure to bring these items along:

1. Your Employment History

Your attorney will be sure to ask about your employment history. Prepare a list of all your previous jobs, and detail every position you've held at your current job. Include in this list your job titles, the responsibilities and duties of each job, and your supervisor(s).

Be sure to include any information, such as commendations or reports of disciplinary actions, that will help establish what kind of employee you were. If you have had bad reviews or other problems prior to the sexual harassment, don't hide them from your attorney.

2. A Copy of Your Personnel File

If possible, try to have a copy of your personnel records from your current job. In some states, employers are only required to let you have access to the file. If your company doesn't allow you to make copies of the documents, go in with a pad and pencil and carefully copy every pertinent document in your file, even if it takes you hours to do so.

Your attorney will want to know what the file contains. List everything, even those things that seem irrelevant to you. Your attorney may see value in things you don't, and small details could become important later on. It could also be valuable to know exactly what's in the file in case either of you suspect your employer of tampering with your records once the case is filed.

3. Company Policy and Procedure Manuals

Your attorney will also want to see copies of your employer's policies and procedures. Attorneys are especially interested in any memos, announcements, or other notices regarding sexual harassment that the company may have posted or distributed to employees.

4. Employment Contracts

You should also give your attorney copies of any agreements you have with your employer. This includes copies of union agreements, employment contracts you've signed, or other evidence of the formal relationship between you and your employer.

5. Personal Evidence

Bring your documentation journal. Be sure to include with it a list of names and phone numbers of everyone with whom you've discussed your situation. This includes co-workers, friends, and counselors who can attest to your personal character. They should have knowledge of what happened and know how the sexual harassment affected you emotionally.

Finally, there's the question of giving your attorney the name of your personal physician, your minister, psychologist or therapist, plus any other health care professional in whom you've confided your situation. These professionals are often in the best position to corroborate your testimony that the sexual harassment has caused you severe emotional stress, but there are other factors to consider as well.

Sometimes attorneys neglect to tell clients that raising medical or mental health issues could waive your right to confidentiality. In some states, you may have to give up your right to privacy if your suit alleges that the sexual harassment has caused you emotional distress. Using mental or emotional distress as a component or basis for your legal complaint may mean that your entire medical and psychiatric records—not just the period during which you were harassed —could be called into question. Ask your attorney for specific advice before you make the decision to include this information.

What Happens Once the Litigation Begins?

Your attorney's role is to help you resolve the complaint you have against your harasser, which may be accomplished without filing a lawsuit on your behalf. You may be able to reach a settlement with your employer even before you go to court, or your case could require a jury trial. Each step will test your patience, strength, and your cooperation.

Be Patient: It Takes Time

Don't expect to resolve your case quickly. A sexual harassment case can take years to litigate. In some states, where there is a backlog of cases, it may take over a year to schedule the first court date. Even if your attorney decides to submit the case to arbitration, rather than pursue a jury trial, you can expect significant time delays.

Each step of the discovery process takes time. Your attorney must decide what information is needed for the case, submit requests for information, allow time for responses, and request additional information or clarification. The time allowed for responses varies according to state law, and this can add months to the negotiations between your attorney and the defendant's attorney.

Be Prepared to Be Involved

Some women incorrectly believe that turning the case over to an attorney means someone else can now fight the battles for them. This is not so. You must still make the major decisions throughout the process.

Plaintiffs in sexual harassment cases often experience personal demands similar to rape victims when they take their cases to trial. Intimate details about your personal life may become an inevitable part of your case. You'll have to tell your story over and over again in exact detail. Be prepared to have your privacy invaded, and to withstand some intensive assaults against your character.

"There are huge emotional demands on the client in a sexual harassment case," says attorney Conni Stamper. "It can be very difficult to hear what your employer has to say about your performance or your character. Sometimes, it almost seems easier for the client to walk away than to put up with the frustrations, the delays, and the constant assaults by the other side. I urge my clients to be realistic about their role in the case. I will need them to help support the strategy we use, and I expect them to be honest with me about the situation. It's vital to winning the case to have the full cooperation of the client." [2]

Remember You Have the Law on Your Side

Even though the legal process itself can sometimes appear to be a labyrinth of delays and maneuverings, the system does work. You have the law on your side. In cases involving discrimination on the basis of sexual harassment, the law puts the burden of proof on the employer to show that the incidents in question never happened or were not meant to harm you. That's often a very difficult thing for the employer to do, given the fact that jurors often feel tremendous personal sympathy for victims of sexual harassment.

Many times, sexual harassment cases never make it to court. Some companies decide that they'd rather offer you a financial settlement than risk the negative publicity of a guilty verdict. Here's where an experienced attorney can be worth the fee many times over by helping you decide if the settlement is fair, and what the long-term consequences are of accepting it. Your attorney can also give you a realistic appraisal of your chances of winning, if you decide to decline the settlement and take the matter on to court.

Prevailing in a lawsuit against your harasser can do more than bring you vindication or financial compensation for the injury you have suffered. It may help you

---

2.   Stamper, Conni L. Interview with author. Spokane, WA, 1992.

close the chapter on a very difficult and demoralizing time in your life, and it can also give encouragement to others to follow your example.

Standing up for your rights in a public forum offers courage to others to come forward and sends a very clear message to harassers in the workplace that they cannot escape the consequences of their actions. It is a message worth sending for yourself, for other victims, and for future generations.

SECTION IV

LOOKING FORWARD

Chapter 17
A NEW WORKPLACE PROTOCOL

Chapter 18
ADVICE TO MEN

Chapter 19
WE'RE ALL IN THIS TOGETHER

Introduction

Long before government agencies and attorneys become involved in sexual harassment cases, we each can take personal responsibility to improve communication and solve our conflicts. Changing behavior begins with an awareness of what we do or don't do that contributes to the ensuing problems of sexual harassment.

By letting your voice be heard in spite of the obstacles, you are taking a responsible step toward stopping sexual harassment. You can also help others become aware of how to prevent conflicts caused by sexual harassment.

In this section you will find guidelines for the new workplace protocol.

Chapter 17

THE NEW WORKPLACE PROTOCOL

Building Professional Relationships

Sexual harassment disrupts relationships and causes much bitterness and divisiveness between men and women. Some women think men will never understand why sexual harassment is an issue. Some men think it's been blown way out of proportion. These issues cause problems for both women and men in the workplace. In this chapter, I'd like to talk specifically about some of the points I consider critical in achieving good working relationships.

As men and women working together, we can't help noticing each other or even being attracted to one another. Some people think the sexual currents between men and women add to the enjoyment of working together. Others find it threatening or demeaning to have their conversations or relationships interpreted in a sexual way at work.

The reality is that sexual behavior just doesn't belong in the workplace, and it's inappropriate for professional relationships. The pleasure you may personally feel about working with someone who attracts you does not give you the right, no matter what your position is in the company, to act on that attraction. Indulging in behavior that makes someone uncomfortable is destructive to relationships. Such behavior could be devastating, not only to your career and job security but to someone else's as well.

If I could offer men one piece of advice on how to avoid accusations of sexual harassment and how to get along in the work place, it would be:

If in doubt... don't. Much of the confusion about sexual harassment could be eliminated if the following simple statement were understood.

Sexual harassment isn't a reaction to sexual signals, it's a conscious act.

Every time you choose to tell an off-color joke, make a personal comment about a person's appearance, or tease someone in a sexual way at work, you engage in behavior that could offend someone. No one wants to face the consequences of being accused of sexual harassment.

To remind you of some guidelines to follow, here is the new workplace protocol from Chapter 5.

The New Workplace Protocol

- Be consistent and treat others consistently.

- Don't barter sexuality for popularity or advancement.

- Dress appropriately for your job without drawing attention to your sexuality.

- Don't use "body language" that others may interpret as sexual.

- Keep personal relationships separate from work relationships.

Chapter 18

ADVICE TO MEN

Communicating at Work

A few points about communicating might help you put things in perspective.

On Paying Compliments

Men often believe that giving compliments to women about their appearance is the best way to foster congenial working relationships, but personal comments can sometimes have the reverse effect. Some women interpret comments about their appearance as sexual 'come-ons'. Others may feel that this kind of attention is sexist, condescending, insulting or even threatening.

Your intentions may be honorable, and your admiration sincere, but don't assume that all women welcome compliments about their appearance. You can express positive feelings and even enhance your working relationship by paying compliments that are work-related. Examples: "You did a nice job on that presentation," or, "You handled yourself well with those clients."

If your relationship with a woman at work is one in which compliments are easily and comfortably exchanged, consider one small adjustment. Instead of saying something with a physical connotation, why not use a more neutral approach? For example: "That's a lovely dress," instead of "That dress really makes you look sexy." The difference in emphasis between these two comments could result in making your colleague feel good rather than feel threatened by you. And unless you have a specific, job-related reason for saying something about a colleague's dress or appearance, consider avoiding the subject entirely.

On Jokes, Cartoons, or Sexual Comments

Even though some women may enjoy jokes, cartoons or stories with sexual overtones, other women find them embarrassing, offensive, and inappropriate for the workplace. It's impossible to tell if you're offending someone, because often women won't say anything.

Sexually-related jokes, posters, or comments offensive to women really don't belong in the workplace at all. They don't contribute to getting the work done, and they carry a high risk of creating what the law refers to as a *hostile working environment*. A hostile working environment interferes with how a person performs his or her job, and it's a prime element in the laws against sexual harassment.

You have two choices: you can either refrain from telling sexually-oriented jokes or stories; or you can ask first, before you run the risk of offending someone. And if someone tells you a joke or story, set the tone by letting them know you don't think it's appropriate for work. Example: "I usually enjoy a good joke, but I don't think it's appropriate to tell sex-related jokes at the office. Why don't we just skip it?"

On Using Endearments

Many women take offense at being called *honey, babe, sweetie,* or other endearments by men at work. In a work environment, such names often make women feel like sex objects, rather than co-workers. Casual informality is one thing, but using terms that are often associated with a personal or sexual relationship can send the wrong signal. If you wouldn't address a male colleague in the same way, it's better to avoid this kind of familiarity at work.

On Physical Contact

A hug or pat on the back may be your way of showing affection or friendship, but some women are very uncomfortable about being touched in this way. Physical contact is not really necessary to maintain a healthy, friendly work relationship, and it often sends the wrong message to a woman, as well as to co-workers. Ask yourself: *Is this appropriate to the situation and to the professional relationship? Could it be misinterpreted by others who didn't know anything about the situation?*

On the Power Relationship

If you're in a supervisory or management position, you have a special responsibility to maintain a professional working relationship with those who work for you. Your authority, and the power you have to make decisions affecting others, places what you do or say in a special context. Women are often highly sensitive to power in the workplace, especially when they feel compromised or threatened by it.

On Asserting Your Masculinity

Some men feel they have a right to treat women as they please, even if their interpretation of what's appropriate behavior may have sexual overtones that could be offensive to others. You may prefer to assert your sexuality to women, but that consitutes poor judgment in the workplace. Relationships at work are different from those in your personal life. If you insist on sexualizing every encounter, you run the very high risk of having your behavior misinterpreted.

On Being Rebuffed

Some men mistakenly believe that when a woman initially says no to a sexual overture, she really means yes or maybe. Even if you personally believe this to be true, this is a dangerous assumption in the workplace.

If a woman tells you she doesn't like something you said or did, listen to what she is saying and respect her point of view. Even if you intended the comment or gesture in an innocent way, ignoring her objection or offending her further is a very risky proposition these days. If she says *no*, hear it as *no*. Don't persist nor repeat what you did or said that offended her.

On Romance

Finding love and romance at work happens all the time, but you ought to keep in mind the risks involved. If you can, keep personal relationships separate from business ones, especially if one of you supervises the work of the other. One of you may consider working in another department or making an adjustment so your work performance is not adversely affected by your personal relationship.

If that's impossible, then at least consider telling your boss or someone in authority about the situation. Aside from possibly offering you advice, that person may help you maintain objectivity on the professional side of the relationship.

What If It Happens To You?

If you find yourself on the receiving end of inappropriate behavior or sexual harassment, don't think of it as a joke or even as a compliment. Sexual harassment is not the same as flirting. It's demeaning to have your work or yourself devalued in this way, and it's rarely seen by men or women as a legitimate way to gain respect on the career track. All employees have a right to work in a discrimination-free environment, and you should insist on being treated with respect.

Chapter 19

WE'RE ALL IN THIS TOGETHER

Looking to the Future

Wᵉ all bring into the workplace our anxieties and vulnerabilities as individuals and as human beings. We seldom leave our beliefs at the door, even when they conflict with the reality of today's modern workplace. That's why sexual harassment continues to challenge us. Our best hope for resolving it is to strive for a work environment that values each individual for his or her contribution. We must continue to learn how to work together.

Blaming all men for sexual harassment would be as unfair as blaming all women for bringing it on themselves. Finding solutions is more important, and solutions must start with individual responsibility.

A Workplace of Respect

The most rewarding (and productive) relationships, especially in today's workplace, are not based on physical attraction or sex, but are built on respect. People who respect one another work better with each other, and they have far fewer problems communicating. Respect is the foundation of trust, and trust is often the deciding factor in motivating people to pull together in times of crisis. Fostering respect for the individual should be part of every organization's mission, but it's not something that can simply be decreed or demanded. Respect is earned, but it can also be taught. We can learn how to respect one another by setting standards for our individual behavior and by practicing those standards:

- Eliminate references to sex or personal issues in our work relationships.

- Stand up to those who demean or challenge us.

- Support others who refuse to accept or allow offensive behavior.

- Say no to sexual advances from co-workers.

- Refuse to participate in an activity or behavior that crosses over the line of being professional to being too personal in the workplace.

- Take personal responsibility for setting an example.

Make Positive Changes: Individually and Collectively

Every time someone says no to sexual harassment, a small step forward is taken. Every time co-workers refuse to engage in sexual repartee or hazing, progress is made. Every time someone tempers his remarks to respect another's privacy or personal beliefs, the workplace environment is improved.

Change won't happen over night, but it can happen if we individually and collectively work toward an enhanced working environment in which sexual harassment plays no part. We are all responsible, women as well as men, for eliminating sexual harassment. All of us have a stake in creating an environment of respect for one another.

Appendix A

List of Organizations to Contact for Information and Support *

The organizations listed below offer a variety of information, programs, and publications on workplace issues. The people I spoke with at a number of these organizations were friendly, eager to help with information, and very well informed. My thanks to the many individuals who expressed such enthusiastic support for the focus of this project.

BUSINESS AND PROFESSIONAL WOMEN/USA
2012 Massachusetts Ave NW
Washington DC 20036
(202) 293-1100

For over 75 years. BPW has conducted research, supported education, and sponsored lobbying for equity and self-sufficiency among working women. Maintains extensive library on issues relating to women and work. Publishes *National Businesswomen* magazine.

---

* NOTE: Addresses and phone numbers of organizations may be subject to change.

9to5, NATIONAL ASSOCIATION OF WORKING WOMEN
614 Superior Avenue NW
Cleveland, OH 44113
(216) 566-9308
1 - (800) 522-0925 National Hotline

Organization dedicated to championing the cause of workers by helping workers deal with workplace issues. Sponsors local chapters and maintains national advice hotline providing legal and counseling referrals. These people really care.

WOMEN'S BUREAU, U.S. DEPARTMENT OF LABOR
200 Constitution Ave NW
Washington DC 20210
(202) 523-6665

Provides statistical and research information on women in the workforce, including training materials, and survey information.

NOW LEGAL DEFENSE AND EDUCATION FUND
99 Hudson Street
New York NY 10013
(212) 925-6635

National organization dealing with political, social, educational, legal, and economic issues in the American workplace. Sponsors a number of publications and re- search programs, including the NOW Legal Defense and Educational Fund.

CENTER FOR RESEARCH ON WOMEN
Memphis State University
Memphis, TN 38152
(901) 678-2770

A computerized information retrieval service and clearinghouse for research focusing on women's studies. Includes several thousand entries of books, journal articles, manuscripts, videotapes and other materials.

NATIONAL ASSOCIATION OF FEMALE EXECUTIVES
127 West 24th, 4th Floor
New York, NY 10011
(212) 645-0770

Publishes national newsletter, provides resource material and related member services including research and education on a variety of issues of interest to working women.

WIDER OPPORTUNITIES FOR WOMEN
1325 G Street NW
Washington DC 20005
(202) 638-3143

Offers resource materials and consulting services focusing on women in nontraditional jobs.

EQUAL EMPLOYMENT OPPORTUNITY COMMISSION
(EEOC)
Office of Communications
1801 L Street NW
Washington DC 220507
(202) 663-4900

Government agency responsible for governing employment practices in the USA. Provides extensive publications on discrimination and equality issues, including periodic reports and surveys of the American workplace, and resource materials for employers.

WOMEN'S LEGAL DEFENSE FUND
1875 Connecticut Ave NW
Washington DC 20009
(202) 986-2600

Sponsors research and provides a variety of publications dealing with advocacy for women and related litigation issues.

NORTHWEST WOMEN'S LAW CENTER
119 South Main, Suite 330
Seattle, WA 98104
(206) 682-9552

Resource center for education, workshops and speakers on a broad range of issues relating to women, equity in employment, and the law. Provides counseling and referral services.

COMMISSION ON ECONOMIC STATUS OF WOMEN
Minnesota State Office Building, Room 85
100 Constitution Avenue
St Paul MN 55155
(612) 296-8590

Conducts research, holds public hearings, and provides reports on issues involving economic status of women. Focuses on discrimination in employment, divorce laws, and child-care issues as they relate to impoverishment of women.

WOMEN FOR RACIAL AND ECONOMIC EQUALITY
198 Broadway
New York NY 10038
(212) 385-1103

Political activist organization dedicated to fighting racism and economic inequality through enactment of Women's Bill of Rights.

APPENDIX B

List of Government Reporting Offices

ALABAMA

EEOC: Birmingham District Office
1900 Third Ave North, #101
Birmingham, AL 35203
(205) 731-0082

State Agency: None at this time

ALASKA

EEOC: No EEOC office

State Agency: Alaska State
Commission for Human Rights
800 A Street, #202
Anchorage, AK 99501
(907) 276-7474

ARIZONA

EEOC: Phoenix District Office
4520 N. Central Ave #300
Phoenix, AZ 85012
(602) 640-5000

State Agency: Arizona Civil
Rights Division
1275 W. Washington St
Phoenix, AZ 85007
(602) 542-5263

RKANSAS

EEOC: Little Rock Area Office
320 W. Capitol Ave #621

Little Rock, AR 72201
(501) 324-5060

State Agency: None at this time

CALIFORNIA

EEOC: Los Angeles District Office
3660 Wilshire Blvd 5th Fl
Los Angeles, CA 90010
(310) 251-7278

Oakland District Office
1333 Broadway, Rm 430
Oakland, CA 94612
(510) 273-7588

State Agency: Department of Fair
Employment and Housing
2014 T St. #210
Sacramento, CA 95814
(916) 739-4621

COLORADO

EEOC: Denver District Office
1845 Sherman St, #201
Denver, CO 80203
(303) 866-1300

State Agency: Colorado Civil
Rights Commission
1560 Broadway,#1050
Denver, CO 80202
(303) 894-2997

CONNECTICUT

EEOC: No EEOC office

State Agency: Connecticut Commission on Human Rights and Opportunities
90 Washington Street
Hartford, CT 06106
(203) 566-4895

DELAWARE

EEOC: No EEOC office

State Agency: Delaware Dept Labor, Anti-Discrimination Section
820 North French Street
Wilmington, DE 19801
(302) 571-3929

DISTRICT OF COLUMBIA

EEOC: Washington Field Office
1801 L Street NW #200
Washington, DC 20507
(202) 663-4264

FLORIDA

EEOC: Miami District Office
2 NE First, 6th Fl
Miami, FL 33132
(305) 536-4491

Tampa Area Office
412 Madison
Tampa, FL 33601
(813) 272-5969

State Agency: Florida Commission on Human Relations
325 John Knox Rd, Bldg F, Rm 240
Tallahassee, FL 32399
(904) 488-7082

GEORGIA

EEOC: Atlanta District Office
75 Piedmont Ave NE
Atlanta, GA 30335

State Agency*: Georgia Office of Fair Employment Practices
156 Tinity Ave SW
Atlanta, GA 30303
(404) 656-1736

*Protections only apply to employees of the state of Georgia; employees of private employers are excluded.

HAWAII

EEOC: Honolulu Office
677 Ala Moana Blvd #405
Honolulu, HI 96813

State Agency: Hawaii Civil Rights Commission
888 Mililani Street, 2nd Fl
Honolulu, HI 96813
(808) 586-8655

IDAHO

EEOC: No EEOC office
State Agency: Idaho Human Rights Commission
450 West State St
Boise, ID 83720
(208) 334-2873

ILLINOIS

EEOC: Chicago District Office
536 S Clark St, 9th Fl
Chicago, IL 60605
(312) 353-2713

State Agency: Illinois Dept
Human Rights
100 W Randolph St, 10th Fl
Chicago, IL 60601
(312) 814-6245

INDIANA

EEOC: Indianapolis District Office
46 E Ohio St, #419
Indianapolis, IN 46204
(317) 226-7212

State Agency: Indiana Civil
Rights Commission
32 E Washington Street
Indianapolis, IN 46204
(317) 232-2612

IOWA

EEOC: No EEOC office

State Agency: Iowa Civil Rights
Commission
211 E Maple Street, 2nd Fl
Des Moines, IA 50319
(515) 281-4121

KANSAS:

EEOC: No EEOC office

State Agency: Kansas
Commission on Human Rights
900 SW Jackson Street

Topeka, KS 66612
(913) 296-3206

KENTUCKY

EEOC: Louisville Office
600 Dr. Martin Luther King Jr. Place
Louisville, KY 40202
(502) 582-6082

State Agency: Kentucky
Commission on Human Rights**
701 West Muhammed Ali Blvd.
Louisville, KY 40201
(502) 588-4024

** *No automatic dual filing with EEOC*

LOUISIANA

EEOC: New Orleans District Office
701 Loyola Ave #600
New Orleans, LA 70113
(504) 589-2329

State Agency: None at this time

MAINE

EEOC: No EEOC office

State Agency: Maine Human
Rights Commission
Statehouse Station 51
Augusta, ME 04333
(207) 289-2326

MARYLAND

EEOC: Baltimore District Office
500 B Abel Wolman Municipal Bldg
Baltimore, MD 21202
(301) 396-5819

State Agency: Maryland
Commission on Human Relations
20 E Franklin Street
Baltimore MD 21202
(301) 333-1715

MASSACHUSETTS

EEOC: Boston Area Office
1 Congress Street
Boston MA 02114
(617) 565-3200

State Agency: MA Commission
Against Discrimination
One Ashburton Place, Rm 601
Boston, MA 02108
(617) 727-3990

MICHIGAN

EEOC: Detroit District Office
477 Michigan Ave, Rm 1540
Detroit, MI 48226
(313) 226-7636

State Agency: Michigan Dept of
Civil Rights
1200 6th Street
Detroit, MI 48226
(313) 256-2613

MINNESOTA

EEOC: Minneapolis Office
220 South Second St, Rm 108
Minneapolis, MN 55401
(612) 370-3330

State Agency: Minnesota Dept of
Human Rights
Seventh Place & Minnesota Street

St. Paul, MN 55101
(612) 296-5665

MISSISSIPPI

EEOC: Jackson Area Office
Cross Roads Complex
207 W Amite St
Jackson, MS 39205
(601) 965-4537

State Agency: None at this time

MISSOURI

EEOC: St. Louis District Office
625 N Euclid, 5th Fl
St. Louis, MO 63108
(314) 425-6585

Kansas City Area Office
911 Walnut, 10th Fl
Kansas City, MO 64106
(816) 426-5773

State Agency: Missouri
Commission on Human Rights
3315 W Truman Blvd
Jefferson City, MO 65102
(314) 751-3325

MONTANA

EEOC: No EEOC office
State Agency: Montana Human
Rights Division
1236 6th Ave
Helena, MT 59624
(406) 444-2884

NEBRASKA

EEOC: No EEOC office

State Agency: Nebraska Equal Employment Opportunity Commission
301 Centennial Mall South, 5th Fl
Lincoln, NE 68509
(402) 471-2024

NEVADA

EEOC: No EEOC office

State Agency: Nevada Equal Rights Commission
1515 E Tropicana, #590
Las Vegas, NV 89158
(702) 486-7161

NEW HAMPSHIRE

EEOC: No EEOC office
State Agency: New Hampshire Human Rights Commission
163 Loudon Road
Concord, NH 03301
(603) 271-2767

NEW JERSEY

EEOC: Newark Area Office
60 Park Place
Newark, NJ 07102
(201) 645-6383

State Agency: New Jersey Division on Civil Rights
31 Clinton Street
Newark, NJ 07102
(201) 648-2700

NEW MEXICO

EEOC: Albuquerque Area Office
505 Marquette NW
Albuquerque, NM 87102
(505) 766-2061

State Agency: New Mexico Human Rights Commission
1596 Pacheco Street
Santa Fe, NM 87502
(505) 827-6838

NEW YORK

EEOC: New York District Office
90 Church St, Room 1501
New York, NY 10007
(212) 264-7161

Buffalo Office
28 Church Street
Buffalo, NY 14202
(716) 846-4441

State Agency: NY State Division of Human Rights
55 West 125th Street
New York, NY 10027
(212) 870-8566

NORTH CAROLINA

EEOC: Greensboro Office
324 W Market
Greensboro, NC 28212
(919) 333-5174

Charlotte District Office
5500 Central Avenue
Charlotte, NC 28212
(704) 567-7100

Raleigh Area Office
1309 Annapolis Dr #500
Raleigh, NC 27608
(919) 856-4064

State Agency:*
North Carolina Office of
Administrative Hearings
P. O. Drawer 27447
Raleigh, NC 27447
(919) 733-0431

State Agency: **North Carolina
Human Relations Commission***
21 West Jones Street
Raleigh, NC 27603
(919) 733-7996

*for state and county employees
and employees of University of NC*

**for employees of private employers*

***No automatic dual filing with
EEOC*

NORTH DAKOTA

EEOC: No EEOC office

State Agency: North Dakota Dept
of Labor
600 East Blvd, State Capitol Bldg
Bismarck, ND 58505
(701) 224-2660

OHIO

EEOC: Cleveland District Office
1375 Euclid Ave, Rm 600
Cleveland, OH 44115
(216) 522-2001

Cincinnati Area Office
525 Vine St, Suite 810
Cincinnati, OH 45202
(513) 684-2851

State Agency: Ohio Civil Rights
Commission
220 Parsons Avenue
Columbus, OH 43215
(614) 466-5928

OKLAHOMA

EEOC: Oklahoma City Area Office
531 Couch Drive
Oklahoma City, OK 73102
(405) 231-4911

State Agency: Oklahoma Human
Rights Commission
2101 N Lincoln Blvd
Oklahoma City, OK 73105
(405) 521-2360

OREGON

EEOC: No EEOC office

State Agency: Oregon Bureau of
Labor and Industry
Civil Rights Division
P. O. Box 800
Portland, OR 97207
(503) 229-6601

PENNSYLVANIA

EEOC: Philadelphia District Office
1421 Cherry St, 10th Fl
Philadelphia, PA 19102
(215) 597-9350

Pittsburgh Area Office
1000 Liberty Ave
Pittsburgh, PA 15222
(412) 644-3444

State Agency: Pennsylvania
Human Rights Commission
2971 North 7th Street
Harrisburg, PA 17110
(717) 787-4412

RHODE ISLAND

EEOC: No EEOC office

State Agency: Rhode Island
Commission for Human Rights
10 Abbott Park Place
Providence, RI 02903
(401) 277-2661

SOUTH CAROLINA

EEOC: Greenville Local Office
15 S Main Street
Greenville, SC 29601
(803) 241-4400

State Agency: South Carolina
Human Affairs Commission
P. O. Box 4490
Columbia, SC 29240
(803) 253-6336

SOUTH DAKOTA

EEOC: No EEOC office

State Agency: South Dakota
Division of Human Rights
500 East Capitol St
Pierre, SD 57501
(605) 773-4493

TENNESSEE

EEOC: Memphis District Office
1407 Union Ave
Memphis, TN 38104
(901) 722-2617

Nashville Area Office
50 Vantage Way
Nashville, TN 37228
(615) 736-5820

State Agency: Tennessee Human
Rights Commission
226 Capitol Blvd, Suite 602
Nashville, TN 37219
(615) 741-5825

TEXAS

EEOC: Houston District Office
1919 Smith, 7th Fl
Houston, TX 77002
(713) 653-3320

Dallas District Office
8303 Elmbrook Dr
Dallas, TX 75247
(214) 767-7015

San Antonio District Office
5410 Fredericksburg Rd
San Antonio, TX 78229
(512) 229-4810

State Agency: Texas
Commission on Human Rights
8100 Cameron Road
Austin, TX 78753
(512) 837-8534

UTAH

EEOC: No EEOC office

State Agency: Utah Industrial Commission, Anti-Discrimination Division
160 East 300 South
Salt Lake City, UT 84111
(801) 530-6801

VERMONT

EEOC: No EEOC office

State Agency: Civil Rights Division Office of Attorney General
109 State Street
Montpelier, VT 05609
(805) 441-3470

State Agency: None at this time

VIRGINIA

EEOC: Richmond Area Office
3600 W Broad St, Rm 229
Richmond, VA 23230
(804) 771-2692

Norfolk Area Office
252 Monticello Ave
Norfolk, VA 23510
(804) 441-3470

State Agency: None at this time

WASHINGTON

EEOC: Seattle District Office
2815 Second Ave, #500
Seattle, WA 98121
(206) 553-0968

State Agency: Washing State Human Rights Commission
Evergreen Plaza Building, Ste 402
711 South Capitol Way
Olympia, WA 98504
(206) 753-6770

WEST VIRGINA

EEOC: No EEOC office

State Agency: West Virginia Human Rights Commission
1321 Plaza East, Room 104/106
Charleston, WV 25301
(304) 348-2616

WISCONSIN

EEOC: Milwaukee District Office
310 W Wisconsin Ave
Milwaukee, WI 53203
(414) 297-1111

State Agency: Wisconsin Equal Rights Division
Dept of Industry, Labor & Human Relations
201 East Washington Ave.
Madison, WI 53708

WYOMING

EEOC: No EEOC Office

State Agency: Wyoming Fair Employment Practice Commission
Job Services Centers (any of 11 locations)
Midwest & Center Streets
Caspar, WY 82602
(308) 234-8650

APPENDIX C

Time Limits for Filing Complaints

Filing procedures may vary. Check with your state agency to confirm the specific time limits and conditions that apply in your state and to your employment situation.

ALABAMA
Alabama has no Fair Employment Practices law.

ALASKA
300 days

ARIZONA
180 days

ARKANSAS
Arkansas has no Fair Employment Practices law.

CALIFORNIA
365 days

COLORADO
180 days

CONNECTICUT
180 days

DELAWARE
90 days

DISTRICT OF COLUMBIA
365 days

FLORIDA
180 days

GEORGIA
Georgia has no Fair Employment Practices law.

HAWAII
180 days

IDAHO
365 days

ILLINOIS
180 days

INDIANA
90 days

IOWA
180 days

KANSAS:
Six months

KENTUCKY
180 days

LOUISIANA
None, but since there is no state agency, EEOC time limits may apply.

MAINE
Six months

MARYLAND
Six months

MASSACHUSETTS
Six months

MICHIGAN
180 days

MINNESOTA
365 days

MISSISSIPPI
Mississippi has no Fair Employment Practices law.

MISSOURI
180 days

MONTANA
180 days, with conditions

NEBRASKA
180 days

NEVADA
180 days

NEW HAMPSHIRE
180 days

NEW JERSEY
None

NEW MEXICO
180 days

NEW YORK
None

NORTH CAROLINA
180 days

NORTH DAKOTA
300 days

OHIO
Six months

OKLAHOMA
180 days

OREGON
365 days

PENNSYLVANIA
180 days

RHODE ISLAND
365 days

SOUTH CAROLINA
180 days

SOUTH DAKOTA
180 days

TENNESSEE
180 days

TEXAS
180 days

UTAH
180 days

VERMONT
Unclear. Statute of limitations (3 years) may apply.

VIRGINIA
None, but since there is no state agency, EEOC time limits may apply.

WASHINGTON
Six months

WEST VIRGINIA
180 days

WISCONSIN
300 days

WYOMING
90 days

Appendix D

Recommended Reading

In addition to the books I've listed here, I've drawn extensively from the surveys and articles published over the years in *Working Woman* magazine. I would like to thank the editors for their persistence and continued vigilance in reporting on issues of interest to working women and men everywhere.

Baer, Jean. *How to Be An Assertive (not aggressive) Woman in Life, Love, and on the Job*. New York: Signet Books, 1976.

Bakos, Susan Crain. *What Men Really Want: Straight Talk From Men About Sex*. St. New York: Martin's Press Paperbacks, December 1991. (Previously published in hardback by St. Martin's in October 1990 under the title, *Dear Superlady of Sex: Men Talk About Their Hidden Desires, Secret Fears, and Number-One Sex Need*.)

Berkowitz, Bob and Roger Gittines. *What Men Won't Tell You But Women Should Know*. New York: William Morrow, 1990.

Bravo, Ellen and Ellen Cassady. *The 9to5 Guide to Combating Sexual Harassment*. New York: John Wiley & Sons, 1992.

Briles, Judith. *Woman to Woman: From Sabotage to Support*. Far Hills, New Jersey: New Horizon Press, 1987.

Brothers, Joyce. *What Every Woman Should Know About Men*. New York: Simon and Schuster, 1981.

Campbell, Bebe Moore. *Successful Women, Angry Men*. New York: Jove Books, 1986.

DeAngelis, Barbara. *Secrets About Men Every Women Should Know*. New York: Delecort Press, 1990.

Druck, Ken with James C. Simmons. *The Secrets Men Keep: Breaking the Silence Barrier*. New York: Doubleday, 1985.

211

Eagly, Alice Hendrickson. *Sex Differences in Social Behavior: A Social Role Interpretation.* Hillsdale, New Jersey: L. Erlbaum Associates, 1987.

Evatt, Cris. *He & She: 60 Significant Differences Between Men and Women.* Berkeley. California: Conari Press, 1992.

Faludi, Susan. *BACKLASH: The Undeclared War Against American Women.* New York: Crown Publishers, Inc., 1991.

Farrell, Warren. *Why Men Are The Way They Are.* New York: Berkeley Press, 1986.

Gilligan, Carol. *In a Different Voice.* Cambridge, Massachusetts: Harvard University Press, 1982.

Gilson, Edith with Susan Kane. *Unnecessary Choices: The Hidden Life of the Executive Woman.* New York: William Morrow, 1987.

Glasc, Inc., J. M. *Sexual Harassment is Bad Business: Training Guide for Professionals.* Spokane, Washington: J.M. Glasc, Inc., 1987.

Gray, John. *Men, Women and Relationships.* Hillborough, Oregon: Beyond Words Publishing, 1990.

Gutek, Barbara A. *Sex and the Workplace: The Impact of Sexual Behavior and Harassment on Women, Men and Organizations.* San Francisco: Jossey-Bass, 1985.

Hardesty, Sarah and Nehama Jacobs. *Success and Betrayal: The Crisis of Women in Corporate America.* New York: Simon & Schuster, 1986.

Hite, Shere. *The Hite Report: Women and Love, A Cultural Revolution in Progress.* New York: Alfred K. Knof, 1987

Johnson, Karen and Tom Ferguson. *Trusting Ourselves: The Sourcebook on Pyschology for Women.* New York: Atlantic Monthly Press, 1990.

Kerr, Barbara A. *Smart Girls, Gifted Women.* Dayton, Ohio: Psychology Press, 1985.

Kirtz, Irma. *Man Talk: A Book for Women Only.* New York: William Morrow, 1986.

Madden, Tara Roth. *Women vs Women: The Uncivil Business War.* New York: Amacom, 1987.

Mainiero, Lisa. *Office Romance: Love, Power & Sex in the Workplace.* New York: Rawson Associates, 1989.

Margolies, Eva. *The Best of Friends, The Worse of Enemies: Women's Hidden Power Over Women.* New York: Doubleday, 1985.

Mason, Marilyn J. *Making Our Lives Our Own.* San Francisco, California: Harper, 1991.

Morgan, Robin. *The Anatomy of Freedom.* Garden City, New York: Anchor Press/Doubleday, 1982.

Nicholson, John. *Men and Women: How Different Are They?* New York: Oxford University Press, 1984.

Norwood, Robin. *Women Who Love Too Much.* New York: Pocket Books, 1985.

Petrocelli, William and Barbara Kate Repa. *Sexual Harassment on the Job: A Step-by-Step Guide for Working Women.* Berkeley, California: Nolo Press, 1992.

Phelps, Stanlee and Nancy Austin. *The Assertive Woman, A New Look.* San Luis Obispo, California: Impact Publishers, 1987.

Rubin, Dr. Lillian. *Just Friends.* New York: Harper & Row, 1985.

Sanford, Linda Tschirhart and Mary Ellen Donovan. *Women & Self-Esteem: Understanding and Improving the Way We Think and Feel About Ourselves.* New York: Anchor Press/Doubleday, 1984.

Tannen, Deborah. *You Just Don't Understand: Women and Men in Conversation,* New York : Random House, 1990.

Tannen, Deborah. *That's Not What I Meant! How Conversational Style Makes or Breaks Relationships.* New York: Random House, 1986.

Tanenbaum, Joe. *Male & Female Realities.* San Marcos, California: Robert Erdmann Publishing, 1990.

Tavris, Carol. *The Mismeasure of Woman.* New York: Harcourt Brace Jovanovich, 1992.

Tavris, Carol and Carole Wade. *The Longest War: Sex Differences in Perspective.* New York: Harcourt Brace Jovanovich, 1984.

Webb, Susan L. *Step Forward! Sexual Harassment in the Workplace—What You Need to Know!* New York: MasterMedia Limited, 1991.

Weiss, Daniel E. ed. *The Great Divide: How Females & Males Really Differ.* New York: Poseidon Press, 1991.

Weitz, Shirley. *Nonverbal Communication.* New York: Oxford University Press, 1979.

Zevnik, Brian L. P. *What Every Manager Must Know to Prevent Sexual Harassment.* Maywood, New Jersey: Alexander Hamilton Institute, Inc., 1991.

INDEX

ABOUT THE AUTHOR

Memory VanHyning has developed, written, and produced management education programs for America's Fortune 500 Companies. She is co-founder of J.M. Glasc, Inc., specialists in video-based training materials for the corporate market.

In 1987, the company produced *Sexual Harassment is Bad Business.* Winner of numerous awards, it is regarded as one of the country's leading awareness videos on sexual harassment and has been featured on a variety of television and radio news programs addressing this issue. VanHyning has authored a number of articles on sexual harassment and management issues for trade publications such as: *Training Magazine, The Personnel News, Communication Briefings,* and *Human Resource Executive.*

A dynamic speaker, writer and business consultant, VanHyning believes that sexual harassment is a matter of personal responsibility, and that men and women must share equally in the development of a new protocol for working together.

ABOUT THE CONTRIBUTORS

Debra S. Borys, Ph. D., is a practicing psychologist, teacher, and lecturer in Los Angeles. She specializes in counseling on the subject of sexual harassment and victimization in general. She is an Assistant Clinical Professor at UCLA Psychology Clinic and is a member of the research faculty at the California School of Professional Psychology. She is a member of numerous psychological organizations.

Tibor Jukelevics, Ph.D., is a practicing psychologist and Director of Center For Family, a counseling group in Los Angeles. His clinical specialties include the treatment of sexual abuse, stress management and health psychology. He is a member of numerous psychological organizations.

219